Hoover Institution Studies 34

Chinese Historiography on
the Revolution of 1911

## Jacket Photo
## *Memorial Tomb of Seventy-Two Martyrs*

This tomb commemorates the Tung Meng Hui martyrs of the abortive Canton Uprising on April 27, 1911, an event much glorified by Nationalists. Seventy-two unidentified bodies (later identified) of participants in the Uprising were buried at the spot later known as the Yellow Flowers Hill, or Huang-hua-kang, in the eastern suburb of metropolitan Canton. Between 1918 and 1923 a Memorial Park consisting of the Tomb and a surrounding garden with elaborate pavillions, placards, and stone inscriptions was constructed on the site by the Nationalists.

Since the Chinese Communists consider the 1911 Revolution an unsuccessful but significant event in the Chinese people's "anti-feudal" and "anti-imperialist" struggles, they have maintained the Memorial Park for mass education and as a tourist attraction.

However, during the Cultural Revolution some Red Guards removed the Statue of Liberty from the top of the Tomb and replaced it with the present twenty-foot high torch. They also scratched off the names of martyrs who became anti-Communist rightists in the Nationalist era or who fled to Taiwan after the founding of the People's Republic. The treatment of the monument, then, reflects the evolving attitudes of both Nationalists and Communists towards the Revolution of 1911.

The photo was taken by the author during his research trip in the summer of 1973.

# CHINESE HISTORIOGRAPHY ON THE REVOLUTION OF 1911

## A Critical Survey and a Selected Bibliography

Winston Wen-sung Hsieh

HOOVER INSTITUTION PRESS
Stanford University
Stanford, California

The Hoover Institution on War, Revolution and Peace, founded at Stanford University in 1919 by the late President Herbert Hoover, is a center for advanced study and research on public and international affairs in the twentieth century. The views expressed in its publications are entirely those of the authors and do not necessarily reflect the views of the staff, officers, or Board of Overseers of the Hoover Institution.

Hoover Institution Studies 34
Standard Book Number 8179-3341-7
Library of Congress Card Number 70-152425
© 1975 by the Board of Trustees of the
    Leland Stanford Junior University
Printed in the United States of America

*Dedicated to the memory of*
*Yin Hai-kuang (1919-1969),*
*whose courageous challenge to political orthodoxies*
*has inspired*
*a generation of Chinese intellectuals*

# CONTENTS

# Foreword

## by Albert Feuerwerker

American study of modern Chinese history and society, which has burgeoned since the end of World War II, should now perhaps be entering upon a new phase. The last two decades have seen an explosion of monographic publication, much of it originating in superb doctoral dissertations which "opened" key subjects for the first time for the English-language reader. There remain immense lacunae, to be sure—for example in the fields of economic and social history—but the nineteenth-century landscape especially, and even the twentieth to a lesser degree, are now studded with significant numbers of pioneering books and articles. In a sense, the coordinates for at least a moderately accurate general mapping of the last two centuries of China's history have been established. Monographic work will and should continue, and because of what has gone before it will be challenged to be both more sophisticated in its analysis and more innovative in its techniques. But there is also the possibility now, as there was not some years ago, to respond to a challenge of a somewhat different order.

At this point what would probably make the most critical contribution to a new leap forward in the quality and influence of our scholarship would be a comprehensive history of modern China—an English-language *t'ung-shih*, if you will—which incorporates in a critical manner the factual and interpretive findings of the myriad recent publications mentioned above. The chief function of such a work no doubt would be to serve as a target for the barbs flung by dissenters, but how immensely important for the progress of knowledge it is that we make explicit where we concur and where we differ, and why. If the likelihood of the immediate appearance of a satisfactory volume constructed along these lines admittedly is small (because the task is so big: its satisfaction would require the incorporation of recent Chinese, Japanese, and European research as well as that done in the United States), the feasibility of partial approaches to the *t'ung–shih* ideal is much greater. Is this not an appropriate time to call, if not for a comprehensive interpretive work by a single historian, then for up-to-date critical examinations of related series of major events, movements, phases, or problems in the development of China's history from the era of Ch'ien-lung to that of Mao Tse-tung?

The Revolution of 1911 is one such major topic whose events and their meaning are now under active reassessment. It appears to me, in any case, that how one interprets the revolutionary movement and the overthrow of the Manchu dynasty has inevitable consequences for one's appraisal of China's subsequent history. To be informed of the relationship between historical writing on the Revolution and the currents of China's modern history is a necessary first step toward undertaking a critical and comprehensive treatment of that event. In addition to surveying this nexus, Dr. Hsieh has provided a carefully selected up-to-date bibliography of the major publications that illustrate his findings.

Ann Arbor, Michigan
September 11, 1972

# Preface

Winston Hsieh broke into print as editor of a student magazine at National Taiwan University. The journal was forced to close in 1956 after it displayed the Statue of Liberty on the cover and obliquely criticized the ruling regime in Taiwan. When I met Winston in 1959, he was one of a talented group of young intellectuals clustered around the late Professor Yin Hai-kuang, whose outspoken essays enlivened the pages of the *Free China Fortnightly,* which was then the champion of Western democracy and intellectual integrity in Taiwan. When I left the island in 1962, the magazine was defunct, its publisher had been sent to prison for ten years, Professor Yin was soon to be hounded from his teaching position at National Taiwan University, and Winston and his friends were to pursue their scholarly careers abroad.

At the time of our first meeting Winston was already engaged in serious scholarly pursuit, working with Shen Yun-lung, Kuo Ting-yee, and Hu Shih of the Academia Sinica, trying to interview as many early Republican leaders as possible. Though only in his mid-twenties, he combined a profound knowledge of recent Chinese history with the cosmopolitan sophistication so evident in this book. Educated entirely on the China Mainland and Taiwan, he could nonetheless discuss Western sociological theory in erudite English studded with Parsonian terminology. I was very favorably impressed as, it seems, was John K. Fairbank, who met Winston on a visit to Taiwan in 1960. Winston was soon enrolled at Harvard.

The contributions of Winston and his friends to American academic life are already impressive. He has brought his encyclopedic knowledge to bear in a tour-de-force review of Howard Boorman's *Biographical Dictionary of Republican China (The Journal of Asian Studies* 31:3 [May 1972], 615-631). Now he has given us a fine analysis of, and guide to, Chinese historiography on the Revolution of 1911. His point of view is independent, nonpartisan, and tough-minded. His labeling the KMT position "orthodox" and the CCP's "neo-orthodox" marks him as a worthy disciple of Professor Yin who, more than the aging and cautious Hu Shih, symbolized the best of May 4th liberalism in Taiwan around 1960. His account documents the way in which nonpartisan scholarship has been smothered by political dogma, but he notes also that even the most confining political milieu cannot destroy the vitality of China's scholarly traditions. He deftly combines a critical yet generous appraisal of what has been accomplished with a keen analysis of what remains to be done. This work is but a sample of things to come, for one book is scarcely an adequate vessel for Winston's cornucopia of information and insights on twentieth-century China. China scholarship in this country can look forward to years of enrichment through his contributions.

Yet it would be fatuous to suggest that Taiwan's loss is America's gain. Even before he left Taiwan, Winston was an active scholar and writer. He was able to enter into disputation with older intellectuals, writing in an elegant *wen-yen* that belied his youth. Taiwan, to say nothing of the People's Republic, needed, and still needs, the critical perspective that men like him can provide. Although acclimatization to an alien culture and language has been easier for him than for those who arrived here less prepared, it still has consumed precious years. His scholarly writings will necessarily be later and fewer than they would have been in his native language. More tragic, as an expatriate scholar rather than a China-based intellectual-citizen, his potential contribution to the solution of modern China's problems is greatly diminished. The gain to American scholarship can never equal the loss to Chinese society. With such bittersweet feelings I conclude this preface to my good friend's book.

John Israel

Charlottesville, Virginia
November 20, 1972

# Acknowledgments

This book grows out of a Chinese youth's fascination with the 1911 Revolution, a subject which was repeatedly taught since my grade-school days, and a historical event in which some of my relatives played a part. I do not know how to repay the debts to my friends in Taiwan. My serious research began there after my college graduation in the late nineteen-fifties, with the assistance and guidance of my colleagues at the Academia Sinica, of the staff of the Nationalist Party Archives, and especially of my mentor Yun-lung Shen, who generously shared with me his wealth of knowledge and his collection on the Revolution.

I am grateful for the honorarium provided by the ACLS-SSRC Joint Committee on Contemporary China, for the substance of this work was first presented, as a special background paper, to the Research Conference on the 1911 Revolution, which was held under the aegis of the Joint Comittee at Wentworth-by-the-Sea, Portsmouth, N.H., in August 1965; for the research fellowships in 1966 and 1969 from the Hoover Institution that made possible the expansion of the work to its present form; for the grants from the Harvard-Yenching Institute which enabled me to make a nineteen-month round the-world research trip in 1966-67, among other assignments to look into the major Chinese collections in Canada, Japan, Taiwan, Hong Kong, Europe, England, and the United States for comprehensive coverage of the subject; and for the summer grant in 1970 from the University of Washington's Far Eastern and Russian Institute, under Dr. George Beckmann's direction, that subsidized the final editing and checking over of the Bibliography.

It would be impossible to acknowledge adequately all the scholarly assistance I have received in preparing this volume from historians, bibliographers, librarians, and editors. I wish nevertheless to express my thanks to the scholars participating in the Wentworth Conference and especially to Mme. Marie-Claire Bergère and Mary Rankin, to Messrs. Martin Bernal, Chang Peng-yüan, John K. Fairbank, Albert Feuerwerker, John Fincher, Michael Gasster, Yoshihiro Hatano, Charles Hedtke, Chuzo Ichiko, Akira Iriye, Marius Jansen, William Johnson, Charlton Lewis, Don Price, John Schrecker, H. Z. Schiffrin, G. William Skinner, Jonathan Spence, Y. C. Wang, and Ernest P. Young for their comments, and to the late Professor Mary C. Wright of Yale University, who was very much the sponsor of this study. Indeed, if this volume is found useful in any sense, special credit goes to Professor Wright, not only because several decades ago she herself collected in China many of the items which are now stored at the Hoover Institution's East Asian Collection and discussed in this volume — items still bearing the stamp of "Wright Project" — but also because her advice and encouragement were of inestimable value in the making of this book.

Among the colleagues at Hoover, I wish to express my thanks to Messrs. Alan H. Belmont, Brien Benson, John T. Ma, Witold Sworakowski, and David Tseng. For other major collections that I have consulted, thanks go to Messrs. Chuzo Ichiko of Toyo Bunko, Eugene Wu of Harvard-Yenching Library, Karl Lo of the University of Washington's Far Eastern Library, and Wang Chi and Warren Tsuneishi of the Library of Congress. I appreciate also the editorial assistance of Mrs. Carole Norton and Mrs. Edna Halperin, for their enthusiasm and skill in making this complicated volume professionally respectable. Finally, my wife, Frances, played an active part in compiling the bibliography and the subject index, and in preparing the manuscript at various stages.

W. H.

Chinese Historiography on
the Revolution of 1911

# ABBREVIATIONS

| | |
|---|---|
| CCP | Chinese Communist Party |
| *HHKM* | *Hsin-hai ko-ming* (The Revolution of 1911; *see* Bibliography entry [2]) |
| *JAS* | *Journal of Asian Studies* |
| KMT | Kuomintang (Chinese Nationalist Party) |
| *KMWH* | *Ko-ming wen-hsien* (Documents on the Revolution [73]) |
| *KSKKK* | *Kuo Shih Kuan kuan-k'an* (Bulletin of the Kuo Shih Kuan [315]) |
| *LSYC* | Li-shih yen-chiu (Journal of Historical Studies [319]) |

# —1—

# Introduction

The phenomenon that political ideology and political myth dominate the writing of history is not uncommon in many parts of the world. This condition is particularly prevalent in China, however, where there has been a long-continued and intimate association of history with politics, where history has often been used by rulers as a source of legitimation, by ministers as a means of remonstrance with their emperors, and by leaders of political movements as an ideological tool. Thus, didactic, public, and essentially political purposes have from time to time outweighed the historian's duty to search out and to present the truth.

In China this political use of history has been reinforced by the traditional emphasis on intellectual orthodoxy, which places great value on "correct" ideas—and among these is the "correct" understanding of history. Heterodox interpretations of past events were to be extirpated. The need to establish and maintain the preferred or acceptable version of history has often led the government to sponsor large-scale enterprises for compiling "standard history," or *cheng-shih*. In addition to the zeal displayed for preserving official documents, assiduous efforts have been devoted to the selection, codification, or suppression of historical data in accordance with the orthodox interpretation. Out of these practices there has grown up in China a formidable tradition of historiography that ranks as one of the oldest and most prolific in the world.[1]

To present a balanced picture, however, we must point out that there were not a few historians who in fact did emphasize such values as historical objectivity and intellectual integrity. In particular, many of them felt the Confucian scholar's moral responsibility to speak out against misgovernment and to use history as a "mirror" to warn and to inspire the monarchical ruler. These attempts served to make of Chinese historiography something more vivid than dull official monologues. Such conflicting principles as the ideal of "truthful records" versus the decency of "appropriate concealment" and as the authoritative application of the criteria of *pao-pien* (praise and blame) by individual historians versus the assumption of "complete objectivity in the collective judgment" of official compilers have lent a peculiar fascination to the development of Chinese historiography.[2] On the other hand, the scholarly commitment certainly brought tension and strain to the tradition of orthodox dominance over historical writing. Thus, in parallel with the massive compilations, there were innumerable instances of persecution of historians, suppression of heretical interpretations, and prohibition or restriction of the circulation of writings that overstepped orthodox lines.

The enormous body of historical works on the Revolution of 1911* that form the subject of the present survey may be viewed as evidence of the vitality of this tradition of Chinese historiography.[3] This vitality is reflected not only in the huge amount of officially and semi-officially sponsored publications on the Revolution pouring out of the Chinese mainland and Taiwan during the past few decades, but also in the intimate, if not inextricable, relationship of the historiography on the Revolution with the political needs and political doctrines of the past half-century. One consequence of this intimacy is the

---

*Since many Chinese writings on the Revolution trace the revolutionary movement to the 1890s, the "Revolution of 1911" will be used in the broader sense in this survey rather than with reference to the revolutionary incident that occurred during the months of 1911-12.

very narrow spectrum of viewpoints represented within the huge output of Chinese writings on the Revolution.

The officially supported doctrines, which arose in the political and intellectual milieu of twentieth-century China, provided the theoretical framework within which major issues on the Revolution were to be explored—and not infrequently distorted or conspicuously ignored.

For analytical purposes, the dominant views on the Revolution are summarized below under two "schools," which are referred to throughout this volume as those of the Orthodox and of the Neo-Orthodox historians. The former, with the official support of the Nationalists, dominated the scene from 1927 to 1949 and still prevails in Taiwan, while the rise of the Neo-Orthodox school coincides with the establishment of political dominance of the mainland by the Communists since 1949. Despite the new features on its Marxist-Leninist jacket, however, Neo-Orthodoxy bears many similarities to the Orthodox doctrines. This phenomenon of continuity reflects in part the effect of intellectual inertia that the long-continued Orthodox domination has imposed upon historical thinking on the subject. Yet, it also points to the fact that both the Orthodox and the Neo-Orthodox schools draw their ideas and their norms, their historians and their methodology from the common intellectual reservoir of twentieth-century China.

## MAJOR CANONS
## OF THE ORTHODOX SCHOOL[4]

Orthodox historians discussed the Revolution of 1911 in terms of the broader definition (see footnote, p. 4). The events of 1911-12, important as they were, are represented as merely one step in the whole process of the revolutionary movement. The "March 29th" uprising in 1911 and the "Second Revolution" in 1913 are regarded as no less significant than the Wuchang Uprising. This view leads us to the first of the major Orthodox canons, namely, the five-stage account of revolutionary history. Each of the five stages, as listed below, is represented by a revolutionary organization of Sun Yat-sen:

1) the Hsing Chung Hui (Revive China Society) period, 1894-1905;
2) the Tung Meng Hui (United League) period, 1905-12;
3) the Kuo Min Tang (Nationalist Party) period, 1912-14;
4) the Chung-hua ko-ming-tang (Chinese Revolutionary Party) period, 1914-19; and
5) the Chung-kuo kuo-min-tang (Chinese Nationalist Party) period, from 1919 on.

Despite the differences in name and methodology of the revolutionary organization in each of the five stages, there have been two essential and unchanging characteristics: the charismatic leadership of Sun Yat-sen and Sun's revolutionary theory — the Three People's Principles. These give rise to the next two canons of the Orthodox interpretation, Sun's leadership and the revolutionary ideology.

According to the Orthodox view, Sun Yat-sen was born a revolutionary and guided the Revolution through all its stages. Sun created the organization and invented the ideology. He guided every revolutionary enterprise, whether personally or in spirit. Even after his death, his immortal spirit guided the revolutionary movement. Sun is portrayed as a dedicated and morally perfect leader possessing vast wisdom and foresight. On the occasions when his revolutionary program failed to materialize, the defeats are attributed either to his followers' lack of will to carry out the program faithfully or to their inability to grasp his ideas. In short, Sun's role in the Chinese Revolution, as depicted in Orthodox writings, is comparable to the Soviet version of Lenin's role in the Bolshevik Revolution.

All the revolutionary ideas and sentiments are interpreted as part of the doctrines of the San Min Chu I, or the Three People's Principles.[5] Since the fuller formulation of Sun's doctrines on nationalism, democracy, and socialism did not emerge until the 1920s, the Orthodox historians place a great emphasis on whatever embryonic signs of these doctrines may be found in the early writings of Sun and his comrades. It is thus a common practice to repeat the story of the "revolutionary-republic vs. constitutionalist-monarchy" debates as carried on in Tokyo in 1906 by the revolutionary organ *Min Pao* and by Liang Ch'i-ch'ao's journal, *Hsin-min ts'ung-pao*. Although the discussions in the *Min Pao* polemics relating to nationalism, democracy, and socialism indeed embodied much of the intellectual ferment of the time, Orthodox historians rarely attempted any critical study of the ideas presented in the *Min Pao* articles. They also tended to ignore the intrinsic contradictions and limitations of Sun's own thinking and to minimize the inconsistencies and conflicting views of Sun and other revolutionaries. In short, the doctrines of the Three People's Principles are accepted as the sacred, infallible guiding ideology of the revolutionary movement. When historians come to evaluate the outcome of the revolutionary endeavor, it is again the Three Principles that are used as the criteria.

Underlying these features of the Orthodox school is a monolithic view of the history of the revolutionary movement. According to this view, the group of revolutionaries under the undisputed leadership of Sun Yat-sen composed the mainstream of the movement. Outside this mainstream there were no significant revolutionary organizations or personalities; and within it there existed no sub-currents, conflicting ideas, or personal disputes.

So far as the Revolution of 1911 itself is concerned, attention is focused upon the predominant role played by Tung Meng Hui members. The Orthodox view maintains that under the spiritual guidance of Sun Yat-sen this group sowed the revolutionary seeds in the minds of the Chinese people—the New Army officers among them; that they staged the Wuchang Uprising; that the nationwide secret network of the Tung Meng Hui was instrumental in causing the secession of the provincial centers from the Manchu empire; that Tung Meng Hui members inaugurated the republican state in China and engineered the abdication of the Manchus; and that any failures and

defeats were due to lack of experience on the part of certain
Tung Meng Hui members.

In the Orthodox version, the roles played by other groups
have often been distorted or even completely ignored. The
revolutionary officers in the New Army in Wuchang are portrayed as local agents of the Tung Meng Hui. The actions of
the constitutionalist gentry are generally ascribed to opportunistic motives: they were forced by circumstances to cooperate
with the revolutionaries but soon surrendered to the camp of
Yüan Shih-k'ai. Although the gentry are occasionally labeled as
the representatives of "feudalistic," "bourgeois," or "traditional" groups or classes, no serious effort has been made by
this school to study their position as a class in relation to the
revolutionary movement. Yüan Shih-k'ai's group and the
Manchu nobility are simply condemned out of hand.


## MAJOR CANONS
## OF NEO-ORTHODOXY[6]


A French historian who had visited the Chinese mainland
on a research trip described the situation of the Neo-Orthodox
domination in a nutshell:

> L'analyse de la révolution par les historiens chinois comporte
> un certain nombre de thèmes fondamentaux, sur lesquels un
> accord unanime est réalisé et dont l'ensemble forme une sorte
> de doctrine officielle qui sert de cadre à toutes les recherches.[7]

To this succinct statement of Marie-Claire Bergère, two
points are to be added. First, these basic themes of the Communist analysis of the Revolution have not yet developed into
a well-knit system of interpretation. Considerable tension and
difficulty arise not only from the gap between Marxist-Leninist
doctrines and historical reality but also from the incompatibility
of the two basic value orientations, the particularistic and the

universalistic trends. Such conflicts in values and tension in interpreting data, to be examined in Chapter IV, contribute some
dynamic and potentially creative element to the otherwise
monotonous outlook of Neo-Orthodoxy.

A second point to be added is that the Communist writers,
despite their alleged antagonistic stand vis-à-vis the Nationalists, have preserved many of the Orthodox views in their post-
1949 writings. To be sure, some works that would have been
branded heretical under Orthodox domination are now published for the first time; and the Marxist-Leninist vocabulary
has become the order of the day. Nevertheless, a careful comparison of the viewpoints on many of the substantial issues in
the Neo-Orthodox publications with those in Orthodox works
reveals a striking similarity, which suggests that, besides
Marxism-Leninism, the Orthodox interpretations form another
major confluent stream for Neo-Orthodoxy. In order to present
the Neo-Orthodox canons, therefore, we may well begin with
a comparison of the features of Communist and Nationalist
writings in general.

At the most generalized level, the similarity of the
Orthodox and the Neo-Orthodox schools may be seen in their
common respect for revolution as a concept. It is beyond the
scope of this study to examine the influence of social Darwin-
ism in twentieth-century China, but "revolution" and concepts
such as "progress" and "change" have generally been held
in high regard by modern Chinese intellectuals. "Anti-
revolutionary" *(fan-ko-ming),* for instance, does not have such an
unsavory connotation to an American as to a Nationalist or to a
Communist.

So far as the revolution of 1911 is concerned, both schools
pay homage to it. Despite the critical attitude toward the
Revolution manifested in early Communist writings, the official Communist line ever since the war has defined it as an "old-
democratic" revolution that represents one important phase of the
revolutionary process of the Chinese people. Both schools recognize that there were missions which the Revolution failed to accomplish. For example, both concede that passing the revolution-

ary regime over to the hands of Yüan Shih-k'ai was a mistake that virtually doomed the first republican experiment in China. Orthodox historians generally attribute this failure to the backwardness of the Chinese people and to Chinese revolutionaries who were not ready to grasp the pioneering ideas of Sun Yat-sen. Neo-Orthodox historians put the same observation in Marxist terms: because of economic conditions, the Chinese bourgeoisie, not yet ready for a fully developed class consciousness, was too weak to assert leadership in the anti-imperialist and anti-feudalistic revolutionary struggle.

Another area of agreement of the two schools is centered around the role played by Sun and his party in the revolutionary movement. Some Communist historians, unlike their Orthodox predecessors, are not reluctant to point up the reformist outlook in Sun's early career and in the initial goal of the Hsing Chung Hui, but they have generally honored Sun as "the forerunner *(hsien-hsing-che)* of the democratic revolutionary movement in China."

As early as the "Resistance War" period, the Communist writings on the Revolution already reflect the political purpose of the Chinese Communist Party (hereafter CCP) to exploit Sun's popular image and to encompass Sun's revolutionary goals in the Communist revolution. Since the take-over in 1949 the Communists have pushed farther in this direction, showering praises upon the "revolutionary forerunner" on occasions like the ninetieth anniversary of his birthday. In fact, the rivalry over Sun's mantle which persisted after Chiang Kai-shek's regime had moved to Taiwan, has resulted in the pouring out, from both the mainland and Taiwan, of voluminous publications on the Revolution in general and on Sun's career in particular.

Nevertheless, the exploiting of Sun's image and the promotion of revolutionary goals went far beyond the political needs of the time. The acceptance of many of the Orthodox views by the Communists was facilitated by the fact that to a considerable extent, the Kuomintang ideology was also exposed to the intellectual impact of Marxism-Leninism. The appeal of the messianic call from Soviet Russia in the wake of the Bolshevik Revolution was by no means confined to the Chinese Communists. And the pervading influence of Marxism-Leninism may be gathered from a quick survey of the historical writings produced during the twenties and thirties. Many non-Marxists, including the Nationalists, were quite used to thinking in such terms as stages of history and social and economic inequality, even though they tended to respond negatively to the teachings on class struggle. In particular, the Leninist doctrine on the aggression of Western imperialists in colonial Asia provided a theoretical framework for many of the nationalistic interpretations on modern Chinese history. Consequently certain of the Orthodox interpretations have been grafted onto Neo-Orthodoxy without difficulty.

To be a true Marxist, however, the Communist historian must explain the Revolution in terms of fundamental trends of economic and social forces rather than on the issue of the personal influence of Sun Yat-sen and other leaders. It is at this point that the Neo-Orthodox school promises to lead us to discoveries beyond the Orthodox horizon. Since the Revolution of 1911 is defined as a bourgeois revolution, one main assignment for Communist writers covering the Revolution is to explain the role in the Revolution of the bourgeoisie as a class. The essence of their argument may be summed up as follows: being exploited by the indigenous feudal forces and foreign capitalism, the Chinese bourgeoisie retained the great potentiality of leading an anti-feudal and anti-imperialist revolution. Under the historical circumstances, however, the Chinese bourgeoisie was differentiated into a "comprador bourgeoisie," which served imperialist interests and was a target of the Revolution; and a "national bourgeoisie," which suffered acutely under the oppression of feudal and imperialist forces and was therefore more revolutionary and nationalistic. While Sun Yat-sen and most other revolutionary leaders came from the national bourgeoisie, the anti-revolutionary forces were supported by the comprador bourgeoisie. Because of its tenuous economic situation, however, even the national bourgeoisie had only the vaguest class consciousness. This helped to account for its compromising attitude toward the antirevolutionary forces and its fear of mobilizing the peasant masses.

Like the Orthodox historians, the Neo-Orthodox writers attach much importance to the role of foreign influence in the course of the revolutionary movement. But in contrast, they interpret the Western impact somewhat unfavorably. Here is thus another area of difference between the two schools. After the rupture of the KMT-CCP alliance in 1928, Orthodox historians tended more and more to shelve their interpretations of imperialist aggression, and showed an inclination to credit the contributions of the West, which ranged from the Western elements in Sun's thought to the dubious foreign aid that had been promised to the revolutionaries before the founding of the Republic. The Neo-Orthodox school, however, has generally observed the Leninist doctrine, paying much attention to the dual role played by Western imperialism. On the one hand, the imperialist powers, with their capitalistic searching for markets and raw materials, had stimulated in China an increase in productivity and an expansion of commerce, and as a by-product had contributed to the emergence of the bourgeoisie. On the other hand, it was also an inhibiting force which crushed the revolutionary will of the bourgeoisie and spoiled the fruit of the Revolution by helping Yüan Shih-k'ai to seize the presidency.

While both schools had devoted much attention to foreign influence, neither made a systematic effort to investigate or to analyze the Japanese impact on the revolutionary movement, even though for several famous scenes in the Orthodox and Neo-Orthodox versions, Japanese names are among the *dramatis personae* and Japanese places provide the setting. The anti-Japanese sentiment among the Chinese, which lingered on after the end of the war, still seems to militate against any scholarly presentation of the Japanese influence on the Revolution.

A last feature of similarity is the faithful observance, on the part of both Orthodox and Neo-Orthodox historians, of the grand tradition of Chinese historiography. This embraces such features as the use of their knowledge and skill to support the reigning orthodoxy, the meticulous attention devoted to the preservation of documents, the compilation under government supervision of vast quantities of records, and, above all, the recognition of value in the didactic, public, and especially political purpose of history writing. All these phenomena taken together form one of the aspects that fit the modern totalitarian order and at the same time attest to the strength of an old tradition in China. Although few scholarly publications on the subject have come out of the mainland since the Cultural Revolution, there is hardly reason to expect the tradition to be discarded in the future, especially since it suits so well the needs of the Chinese Communist state.

## GENERAL PLAN OF THE SURVEY

However far the historical study of the Revolution may advance in the future in terms of interpretation and presentation, the voluminous writings produced during the 1911- 72 period will continue to serve as the major fountain of information. Since political authorities both on the mainland and on Taiwan have explored the archival collections that survived the civil war decades, and since the witnesses to the revolutionary events have either passed away or have entered their declining years, it is unlikely that any substantial amount of new material will be found outside this body of literature produced during the past half-century. It would therefore seem all the more advisable that researchers should become familiar not only with the nature of this material but also with the specific political and ideological forces that created the milieu for the preparation of these works.

This book, therefore, is designed not merely as a bibliographic survey, although attention has indeed been paid to the problems concerning revision of texts, differences among editions, and the selection and compilation of documents. The volume is essentially a historical and historiographical essay intended to highlight the representative works and the major trends of Chinese historical writings on the Revolution. And it is in the perspective of the old tradition of Chinese historiography and in the more specific context of the political and intellectual history of twentieth-century China that various trends of Chinese writings on the Revolution are presented and interpreted in this volume. Such a plan seems to serve two purposes in addition to the study of the Revolution. First, by illuminating one major, recent manifestation of the formidable tradition of Chinese historiography, this survey should contribute to the understanding of Chinese historiography in general. Second, as a faithful reflection of the political and ideological conditions of the Republican and Communist eras, the writings on the Revolution offer a great opportunity for the observation of the political history of twentieth-century China.

While the survey of the development of the Orthodox school extends as far as to the most recent development in Taiwan in 1972, the examination of the Neo-Orthodox writings ends essentially with 1966, when the flow of materials from the Chinese mainland was abruptly halted by the Cultural Revolution, and from which point no significant publication has emerged. As the study has been organized, one chapter is devoted to a survey of the early writings (1902-26), one to the period of Orthodox domination (1927-49), one to Neo-Orthodox domination (since 1950), and one to the development in Taiwan (since 1945).

In order to highlight future research possibilities in the study of the Revolution, the concluding chapter offers a general evaluation of the merits and limitations of Chinese historiography on the Revolution. To add to the possible value of the volume as a research tool, a selected bibliography of Chinese publications related to the Revolution is provided as the second major part of this volume, with the Hoover call number given in parentheses for those entries that are to be found in the Hoover East Asian Collection.

## — 2 —

# Early Writings on
# the Revolution, 1902-27

The early writings on the Revolution deserve our attention mainly for two reasons. First, these writings, though too close to the scene to offer a proper perspective, preserve much contemporary information for the use of later historians. Second, in the years before the rise of Orthodox domination, writers on the Revolution enjoyed a large amount of freedom to express independent views. The variety of viewpoints presented in their works appears in retrospect a rare phenomenon when contrasted to the writings of the later periods of Orthodox and Neo-Orthodox domination.

Chinese writings on the revolutionary movement appeared as early as the decade before 1911. Besides the ''revolutionary histories'' in the ephemeral Chinese student journals published abroad,[8] a few books (presumably printed in the foreign concessions of Shanghai or of other treaty ports) gave accounts of such sensational cases as the martyrdom of the female revolutionary Ch'iu Chin,[9] and the ''Su Pao case'' — the lawsuit involving the slighting of the Emperor Kuang-hsü by Chang Ping-lin and Tsou Jung.[10]

While these accounts were written mainly for revolutionary propaganda or journalistic purposes, a more serious and more influential work published before 1911 was the Chinese translation of part of the Japanese autobiography of Miyazaki Torazo, a Japanese comrade of Sun Yat-sen.[11] The Chinese version, entitled *Ta ko-ming-chia Sun I-hsien* (Sun Yat-sen the great revolutionary),[12] had a wide circulation before it was banned by the Ch'ing government. Even afterward it probably continued to circulate among Chinese students in the treaty ports and abroad. Because the book contains Miyazaki's first-hand account of many of Sun's earlier activities, and because of the author's favorable attitude toward Sun, this book has become one of the principal sources for Orthodox historical writings.

The well-known *Kidnapped in London*, which was the earliest of Sun's own accounts to be written with any degree of seriousness, was not translated into Chinese until after the Wuchang Uprising in 1911 [213]. In this work Sun gives an account of his early revolutionary career that is quite different from the version later accepted in the Orthodox view. However, Sun subsequently disavowed the account he himself had given in the book. And the publication in 1930 of Lo Chia-lun's critical study of the kidnap incident [178] delivered the *coup de grâce* to the book as a reliable source.[13]

During the months following the Wuchang Uprising, there developed a vogue for writings on the Revolution. Reports and biographical accounts of revolutionary leaders appeared not only in the *Min-li pao*,[14] the newspaper run by revolutionists in Shanghai, but also in many non-political journals.[15] On the whole, the contemporary information they recorded has been a valuable source for later historians. A representative sample of such works is Kuo Hsiao-ch'eng, *Chung-kuo ko-ming chi-shih-pen-mo* (A full account of the Chinese Revolution) [145].

Among the works of a documentary nature[16] is the *Kung-ho kuan-chien lu* (The key documents to the founding of the Republic), which contains many well selected materials on the negotiations conducted between representatives of the revolutionists and of Yüan's group in Shanghai in 1911-12 [264]. As for monographical writings, the impression I gathered from an examination of some three dozen items produced in the brief period is that they are generally descriptive rather than analytical, facile rather than penetrating.[17] The more valuable items among them are accounts by surviving revolutionaries about their martyred comrades[18] and hitherto unpublished anecdotes of the revolutionary movement.[19]

While a few works do condemn the uprisings,[20] most of the available writings of the period describe the Revolution in a favorable tone. A great majority of them deal with events in the narrow sense of the Revolution and view the conflicts as mainly a racial issue. They either stress Manchu brutality in the past or advance the ideal of self-government by Chinese. A typical example of these efforts is the very popular eleven-volume work entitled *Man-i hua-hsia shih-mo-chi* (An account of the Manchu barbarian's rule of China) [275].

Systematic interpretations from the revolutionist side appeared somewhat late in the period we are discussing. In response to the demands of the revolutionaries, a Bureau for the Investigation of Revolutionary Deeds, inaugurated in 1912, had as its main function the collection of information on the deeds of revolutionary participants and martyrs.[21] Such information could have contributed to the study of the Revolution had the bureau not been abolished the following year by Yüan Shih-k'ai. It was only after Yüan had crushed the "Second Revolution" in 1913 that Sun and his followers began to reflect seriously on the course of the Revolution and to develop the set of specific views that were to become the basis for Orthodox interpretation. Life in exile in Japan[22] and the bitter experiences of warlord politics[23] made Sun look nostalgically upon the years of his revolutionary past. In this frame of mind and amid the intellectual and political circumstances of the period, he saw a need for a new interpretation of the Revolution. The Chinese public, having witnessed the melodramatic episodes of Yüan Shih-k'ai and other warlords, regarded the Revolution as a complete failure. This general disillusionment is evident from the newspapers and popular journals of the period. In order to create a new image for the Revolution, Sun pointed out the positive aspects of the

Revolution. As for its unaccomplished missions, he stressed that the kind of ideological dedication and correct leadership that were exemplified by his own career and that had led to the downfall of the Manchu throne would undoubtedly guarantee the eventual success of revolutionary endeavor. In such a way, the Revolution of 1911 was depicted by Sun as merely one stage of a long revolutionary process.

This approach served the purpose of answering Sun's political needs. Generally speaking, the revolutionaries, lacking financial and military support, had been able to base their claim to political power only on their past contributions to the founding of the Republic. What made Sun's need for a fortified claim to leadership particularly urgent, however, was the challenge to his leadership from his own ranks. Many revolutionaries had deserted him,[24] had cooperated with the hostile warlords,[25] or had competed with his group for influence in the overseas Chinese communities.[26] These circumstances spurred Sun's group to claim his undisputed leadership of and seniority in the whole revolutionary movement.

The group's view of revolutionary history was crystallized in 1918 in Sun's autobiographical work, *Yu-chih ching-ch'eng* (Where there is a will there is a way), originally written as the concluding chapter of his program for China's ideological revolution and re-construction. This work, which was soon published in a single volume under the new title *Ko-ming yüan-ch'i* (The origin of the Revolution) [210], has been accepted ever since by Orthodox historians as the most authoritative of Sun's accounts of the revolutionary movement. In 1923 Sun published another work, entitled *Chung-kuo ko-ming shih* (A history of the Chinese Revolution), in which his basic views on the revolution were formulated in a more articulate and coherent way [209]. These two works were to guide not only the Orthodox interpretation of specific events but also the evaluation of the Revolution as a whole.

In these works Sun presented himself as the only pioneer of the revolutionary movement: "From the date when I dedicated myself to the revolutionary cause . . . to the founding of the Tung Meng Hui . . . , revolution was almost the business of myself alone. Thus, it is a simple story and I can easily recollect the activities of those few who assisted me materially.''[27] Here there is little room for giving credit to other revolutionary pioneers.

These works suggest that the Tung Meng Hui was created by Sun single-handedly. In order to minimize the initiative and contributions of Huang Hsing and other Chinese student-revolutionaries in Japan, Sun stressed that the formation of the Tung Meng Hui was not a result of the series of meetings with Huang and others in Tokyo in mid-1905. These meetings, he asserted, were but the fourth conference of the Tung Meng Hui and had been preceded by three other conferences he had called a few months earlier in Brussels, Berlin, and Paris.

Sun maintained that the Wuchang Uprising had been conducted by his faithful Tung Meng Hui members according to his revolutionary principles. Moreover, the uprising was greatly aided during the most critical weeks by the neutrality of the foreign powers, whose envoys in Wuchang accepted the revolutionaries as the followers of Sun. In short, Sun's role was indispensable in the whole process.

When Sun turned to evaluate the Revolution as a whole, he regarded it as both legitimate and necessary because ''it corresponded with the heavenly mandate, with public opinion, with the direction of the current tides of world affairs and the needs of mankind.''[28] Moreover, he added an activist element to his interpretation of the Revolution. He felt it was his own single-minded dedication and persistent effort that had led to the achievement of what had initially seemed an impossible task—the overthrow of the Manchu dynasty and the abolition of the monarchical tradition in China. As for the defeats of other parts of his revolutionary program, he attributed these mainly to the failure of his comrades to dedicate themselves to the program he had set up.

This interpretation was suited to the intellectual atmosphere of the May Fourth period. The general desire for change and progress, as manifested in the writings of the new intelligentsia, was paralleled by a tendency toward cultural and political activism—a tendency leading to the belief that human endeavor could change and shape the course of history. Understandably, Sun's activistic view of revolutionary history was generally well accepted by "progressive" intellectual circles.

In addition to publishing Sun's works, his group founded journals and publishing houses to promote their ideas[29] and sponsored certain projects to collect materials on the revolutionary movement.[30] One result of these projects was the *Huang-hua-kang ch'i-shih-erh-lieh-shih shih-lüeh* (Biographical accounts of the seventy-two martyrs on Yellow-Flower Hill) [137]. This story of the tragic uprising in Canton fits much more comfortably than does the Wuchang Uprising into the framework of Sun's interpretation because the Canton episode was conducted mainly by Tung Meng Hui members, without the active participation of the New Army officers and the constitutionalist gentry. Sun's group exalted the abortive attempt in Canton in terms similar to, if not more glowing than, those used to describe the successful Wuchang Uprising. Thus, it became a common exercise of the Orthodox historians to demonstrate the necessity of the Canton martyrdom to the success of the Wuchang Uprising; but few efforts have been made to investigate the actual relationship between the two uprisings in terms of organization, program, and personal ties.

While the chaos of the warlord period did not provide great security for intellectuals and scholars, neither was it possible to impose a set of orthodox interpretations on the historians. We have pointed out the general disillusionment with respect to the Revolution, an attitude Sun was trying to modify. Understandably, few Chinese warlords of the period turned to this tarnished image of the Revolution as a source of legitimation or political self-aggrandizement. Further, the unstable tenure and the limited power of warlords made impossible the rise of any effective official dominance over historical thinking. Under such circumstances, with the absence of official domination, there were no serious obstacles to the emergence of publications expressing views at odds with those of Sun's group.

One widely acclaimed work published in this period was Ku Chung-hsiu's *Chung-hua min-kuo k'ai-kuo shih* (A history of the founding of the Republic of China) [139]. Based on the author's experiences, and on the documents he had acquired as a participant in the Provisional Government in Nanking during 1911-12, this reasonably objective, though somewhat tedious, account has been regarded as an authoritative source on the formation and development of the Provisional Government. As an active constitutionalist in the late Ch'ing period, Ku was able to give information generally omitted in later writings concerning the part played by the gentry-constitutionalists during the 1911-12 period.

Two valuable works by the revolutionaries T'ao Ch'eng-chang and Sung Chiao-jen were published posthumously in the same period. T'ao's book, *Che-an chi-lüeh* (A succinct account of the [Revolutionary] incidents in Chekiang) [223] is based upon his intimate knowledge of the anti-Manchu secret societies in general and of the Kuang Fu Hui (Society for the Restoration [of China]) in particular. His account of the activities of these societies, which were mostly independent from and earlier than the Tung Meng Hui, gives us a quite different perspective of the revolutionary movement from that rendered by Sun's school. T'ao's prejudices against Sun certainly affected his view of Sun's role in the revolutionary movement, but because of the scarcity of available materials on the situation in Chekiang and on the Kuang Fu Hui and other secret societies, historians have treasured the book as a classic on these subjects.

Sung Chiao-jen's diary, under the title of *Wo chih li-shih* (An account of my life) [217], covering his revolutionary career during the period 1904-07, is an important source for the study of the Tung Meng Hui. His account of the formation of the Tung Meng Hui and of the complaints of Huang Hsing and others against Sun's high-handed manner contrasts sharply

with Sun's more publicized version of the history of the Tung
Meng Hui. The discussions of political issues and theories in
the diaries also provide precious clues for the investigation of
the thinking of the Chinese student-intelligentsia in Tokyo in
the mid-1900s.

A monumental work on the revolution, Shang Ping-ho's *Hsin-
jen ch'un-ch'iu* (Spring and autumn annals: 1911-1912), made its
appearance in 1924 [202]. Shang's work is the only comprehensive
account of the Revolution offered by an author whose views differ
in many major respects from those of the Orthodox school. One of
the author's original contributions is that instead of interpreting
the revolutionary activities as a monolithic movement sponsored
from the center by the Tung Meng Hui, he highlights regional
developments and local differences and presents a nationwide, or
empire-wide, survey of the regional situations, province by province, including Manchuria, Outer Mongolia, and Tibet. Among
the provinces, he gives top priority to developments in Szechwan,
where mass demonstrations against the railway policy of the
Ch'ing government were staged on the eve of the Revolution, and
in Hupeh, the first province to secede from the Manchu empire.
This is in contrast to the primary importance in revolutionary
history given to Kwangtung by Sun Yat-sen's group.

While twenty-two *chüan* are devoted to provincial developments, Shang gives only two *chüan* to the history of the
revolutionary movement. Here he traces the movement to the
Taipings, the anti-Manchu secret societies in the early Ch'ing,
and even to the anti-Mongol uprisings that led to the downfall
of the Yuan dynasty in the late thirteenth century. In Shang's
treatment, not only is Sun's role in the movement dwarfed,
but the basic revolutionary cause is reduced to the simple issue
of racial conflict.

Although the author presents much information on
revolutionary activities, he is concerned primarily with the
maintenance of legitimacy, order, and national unity. This concern leads him to view the revolution, on the whole, as an
abnormal phenomenon; and his presentation of events clearly
reflects this attitude. He ends each of his accounts of develop-

ments in the provinces not with the overthrow of Manchu rule but with the restoration of orderly government, which in most cases was not controlled by the revolutionaries. Likewise, he ends the story of the revolutionary movement not with the abdication of the Manchu throne in 1912 but with the defeat of Sun's group by Yüan Shih-k'ai in 1913. If we may judge from some of his remarks on the policies of the Ch'ing government and of Yüan, Shang did not have a deep commitment to the Manchu court nor to Yüan's regime, as some Orthodox historians have charged.[31] Rather, he was a typical conservative, committed to the maintenance of legitimate government and social order. He deliberately used in his title the phrase "spring and autumn annals" *(ch'un-ch'iu),* from the classic compiled by Confucius, to emphasize his primary concern for legitimacy and order.

Shang's work, to which he devoted some thirteen years of research, is a fine example of the application of the skills and standards of traditional Chinese historians to the study of the Revolution. His purpose is essentially to provide an encyclopedic coverage of facts rather than a theoretical generalization, and his presentation is descriptive rather than analytical. The author consciously models his literary style after that of Ssu-ma Ch'ien.[32] And he interprets revolutionary changes in terms of the influence of individuals and of personal virtues rather than in the context of economic and institutional developments.

Historians who held a still more traditional outlook viewed the events of 1911-12 as but another dynastic change, albeit complicated by the racial issue, in the long history of the Sinocentric empire. Some of them, though lamenting the misbehavior of the last rulers of the Ch'ing, chose to show their unshakable loyalty to the lost dynasty by condemning the changes. A typical example of the work of such historians is Wu Tzu-hsiu's *Hsin-hai hsün-nan chi* (Martyrdom in 1911) — the martyrs being Ch'ing officials, not revolutionaries [267]. In the preface written by Wang Hsien-ch'ien, a well-known Confucian scholar, the downfall of the Ch'ing dynasty is attributed to two crucial errors of the Manchu court. First, the introduction of modern reforms in schools and in the army had resulted in the bringing together of the "uncultivated commoners." Still worse had been the policy of sending students abroad, where they acquired heretic ideas. Second, the court had neglected the traditional combination of punishment and reward in administration. Wang maintains the court should have punished Governor-General Jui-cheng for fleeing his post in Wuchang during the Uprising. Once the court had failed to take action against Jui-cheng, it could hardly have imposed discipline on other provincial officials. Both the compiler and the preface writer were Chinese, but they saw no racial conflict involved. Writers like them viewed the Revolution, at best, as another dynastic change or, at worst, as a series of military coups.

To sum up, several points emerge from this survey of the early historical writings. First, the works produced before and during the 1911-12 period, though too close to the events to offer anything beyond descriptive accounts, have preserved much contemporary information on the Revolution. Second, the decade following the 1913 exile to Japan of Sun Yat-sen and his comrades was in a sense the formative period of the Orthodox version of the Revolution. This school of interpretation, stemming from the political needs of Sun's group, was encouraged by the intellectual currents of the May Fourth period. Third, other works of the period express a great variety of viewpoints: those of revolutionists other than Sun, of the constitutionalists, of the conservatives, and of the traditionalists. This variety of viewpoints suggests what the Chinese historians might potentially have accomplished if this period had not been followed by forty years of Orthodox domination.

# Domination of the
# Orthodox School, 1928-49

Following the Northern Expedition of the Nationalist forces, Sun Yat-sen's school of interpretation was exalted to a position of orthodoxy, which dominated historical writings on the Revolution in China in the 1928-49 period. The canons of the Orthodox school form a doctrinal framework for the historical interpretation of the Revolution under Nationalist rule. Among the Orthodox writers there were, of course, differences and disputes and even signs of development in historical thinking, but all within this framework. It was also these canons that were used as the criteria for charges of heterodoxy against certain works during the years of Orthodox domination.

## THE RISE OF
## ORTHODOX DOMINATION, 1928-37

In order to provide a legitimate basis for the launching of the Northern Expedition and for the subsequent Nationalist rule over China, the Kuomintang advanced the theory that the "national will" was embodied in the Chinese Nationalist Party (from the Chinese version of which the name "Kuomintang" was derived), a party which was carrying out the "National Revolution" *(Kuo-min ko-ming)* and which, at the previous stages of the revolutionary movement, had already achieved such revolutionary tasks as the liberation of the Chinese people from the yoke of the Manchus and the elimination of the warlords. This theory thus identified the history of the revolutionary movement with that of the party. Sun Yat-sen's story of the Revolution, which best served the party interest, was therefore raised to an ideological position as sacred as that of the Three People's Principles. Owing to the Nationalist ideological stance, which was much more militant and intolerant in the late 1920s than in the thirties and forties, the Orthodox version of the Revolution left a distinct mark on the historical writings produced in this period.

A general impression of the dominance of the Orthodox view may be gathered from a quick survey of historical publications of the period. Not only did the Orthodox view prevail in history textbooks for all levels of schools but it was reflected in even as serious a work as Li Chien-nung's survey of modern Chinese history.[33]

Those writings that put forward heretic views were condemned. Many of them, such as the writings of Chang Huang-ch'i,[34] were never published during the period of Orthodox domination. Others were suppressed, a notorious example being the confiscation in 1928 of the published but as yet largely uncirculated copies of *Ch'ing-shih-kao* (A draft history of the ch'ing dynasty [24]. Some works, such as *Nan-t'ung Chang Chi-chih hsien-sheng chuan-chi* (A biography of Chang Ch'ien from Nantung) [12], had either to delete the controversial evidence or to interpret it in a way that would not mar the image of the revolutionary leaders.

Beginning in late 1926, the rise of Orthodox dominance was heralded by a proliferation of publications on the Revolution. However, unlike the publications of 1912, the great majority of these writings merely repeated the Orthodox version. Sun Yat-sen's revolutionary career in particular became the subject of many historical and biographical works[35] that were to become part of the Nationalist tradition of the personality cult. A typical example of such a study is that of Hu

Ch'ü-fei, *Sun Chung-shan hsien-sheng chuan* (A biography of Sun Yat-sen), a carefully compiled work based strictly on officially approved materials, with citation of sources for almost every statement [113]. Some of the refined editions of Sun's writings and pronouncements produced during this decade remain a useful reference for the study of the Revolution.[36]

One feature of the period is that, with the brilliant exception of Lo Chia-lun's study of the London kidnap incident [178], the leading works on the history of the Revolution were written not by professional historians but by surviving participants. The following titles furnish a few examples of such works:

*Chung-kuo Kuo-min-tang shih-kao* (Draft history of the Chinese Nationalist Party, hereafter *Draft History*) [237]. This monumental work, often regarded as a "classic" by the Orthodox school, was compiled by Tsou Lu, a revolutionary from Kwangtung[37] who had actively participated in the previously mentioned project of collecting materials on the revolutionary movement. Since its publication in 1929 this work has not been surpassed in comprehensiveness and influence by other works of its kind.[38]

*Hsing-chung-hui ko-ming shih-yao* (Essentials of the revolutionary history of the Hsing Chung Hui) [34]. This most authoritative account of the activities of the Hsing Chung Hui was rendered by Ch'en Shao-pai, one of Sun's comrades from the days when Sun attended medical school in Hong Kong.

*Chung-hua-min-kuo k'ai-kuo-ch'ien ko-ming-shih* (A history of the revolution [-ary movement] preceding the founding of the Republic of China) [82]. This work by Feng Tzu-yu was the first attempt by a surviving participant to give a detailed survey of the entire revolutionary movement. Because Feng was one of the few intellectuals who had joined the Hsin Chung Hui and who had lived long enough to tell the story, his writings on the Hsing Chung Hui have been accepted as a valuable source on the subject.[39] Moreover, as director in 1911-12 of the Bureau for the Investigation of Revolutionary Deeds,[40] Feng had access to many original documents that were later destroyed. For these reasons, Feng was regarded almost as a living encyclopedia of the history of the revolutionary movement.

The more significant aspect of Feng's book is that many of its merits and shortcomings are typical of the writings of the revolutionist historians in general. Such writings based mainly on personal experiences certainly provide a wealth of first-hand information for the study of the revolutionary movement. And like the work of many other revolutionist historians, Feng's writings reflect his unquestioned eagerness to have the revolutionary movement recorded. His enthusiasm, however, often leads him to exaggerate the significance of many incidents in the movement, especially of those in which he himself took part. Feng's major weakness is his lack of the discipline necessary for serious historical writing. He does not systematically cite the sources for his data. On many occasions the reader has no way to distinguish between facts and opinions or speculations. Discrepancies and errors are numerous.

These reservations from a scholarly viewpoint do not, however, imply any deprecation of the merit or the influence of these works. As a matter of fact, they did stimulate historical interest in the Revolution during that decade and they remain today as primary sources for the study of the revolutionary movement.

The first major attempt at a comprehensive treatment of the military aspect of the Revolution was also produced by a young participant in the Revolution, Wen Ti (also known as Wen Kung-chih), whose *Tsui-chin san-shih-nien Chung-kuo chün-shih-shih* (A military history of modern China: 1894-1927) includes accounts of the military takeover in most of the provinces in 1911-12 [253].

Another feature of the writings of this period is the emergence of conflicting accounts within the general framework of the Orthodox interpretation. These controversies were deeply imbedded in political rivalries that existed among the Nationalists themselves. For example, since many Cantonese politicians could lay claim to positions of power only on the basis of their seniority in the revolutionary movement, their accounts of the Revolution tended to highlight their close association with Sun Yat-sen and the prominent role the Cantonese had played in the whole movement. One such account is the *Ko-ming hsien-lieh chi-nien chuan-k'an* (A special anthology in commemoration of revolutionary martyrs), [41] published in 1932 by the Southwestern Bureau of the Kuomintang, which was then challenging the authority of the Nanking government.

In order to lend a new perspective to the important role that Kwangtung had played in the revolutionary movement, Hu Han-min's group in 1927-28 even suggested a "geographical" approach to the interpretation of revolutionary history.[42] They emphasized that the reasons for the achievements and failures of the Revolution could be properly grasped only in terms of political geography.

The group divided power centers in China into three geographical areas along the three major rivers: the Pearl River area in southern China, the Yangtze River area in central China, and the Yellow River area in northern China. According to this group, the history of Sun Yat-sen's revolutionary endeavor up to the "March 29" Uprising in 1911 shows that the revolutionary movement aimed at controlling the Pearl River area while using the overseas Chinese communities as operational bases. The revolution in the second period, i.e., after the "March 29" Uprising in 1911 and before the launching of the Northern Expedition in 1926, was aimed at controlling the Yangtze valley while using as a base the Pearl River valley. In the present, third, period, the revolutionary forces moved farther north to the Yellow River valley while using as bases the Pearl River and the Yangtze areas. To ensure the success of the revolutionary movement during this period, it was necessary, according to their scheme, to unite the Yangtze area with the Pearl River area for the following reason: the regional traits of the Yangtze valley people, manifested in a lack of aggressiveness, an excessive desire for a comfortable life, an economy of consumption and a readiness to compromise, had to be compensated for by the assumed characteristics of the Cantonese, which are drive, initiative, productivity, and aggressiveness. Had this approach been further advanced, it might have enriched the Orthodox interpretation of the Revolution; but because of its clear implication that the Cantonese should play a leading role in the revolutionary enterprises, it was not encouraged by other groups.

In the writings on the Revolution, however, the general enhancement of the Cantonese role had by 1928 already reached such proportions that an old Japanese comrade of Sun felt it necessary to advise Feng Tzu-yu not to overemphasize the role of the Cantonese and not to ignore the role played by Huang Hsing and other revolutionaries in various areas outside of Kwangtung.[43]

Other groups in power also paid great attention to their own image in revolutionary history. A good example was the effort to create a new image of Ch'en Ch'i-mei, a revolutionary from the lower Yangtze delta who was assassinated by an agent of Yüan Shih-k'ai. As a sworn brother of Chiang Kai-shek and an uncle of the Ch'en brothers who headed the rising CC clique, Ch'en Ch'i-mei was now worshiped as a great revolutionary martyr,[44] and Sun's comments on Ch'en were much publicized: "The martyr's contribution to the revolutionary movement was as great as that of Huang Hsing."[45]

Such a difference of emphasis within the framework of the Orthodox version, which stemmed from regional or personal interests, could possibly have led to new angles of interpretation and thus enriched the Orthodox version. In the case of Ch'en Ch'i-mei, for example, his experiences as the revolutionary governor of Shanghai in 1911-12 might have provided an interesting case for the study of class conflict in the Revolution. Rumors, true or false, of Ch'en's generous assistance to the poor made him popular among the lower classes in Shanghai.[46] Indeed, most of the volunteers who enlisted in the revolutionary army under his command were members of the lower classes.[47] In the meantime, his intimate connection with the gangster societies was viewed as scandalous by the gentry scholar group.[48] A careful study of the conflicts involving different classes, not necessarily from the Marxist point of view, might have rendered much insight to our own understanding of the Revolution. But the writers on Ch'en's revolutionary career rarely go beyond the eulogy of the stereotype.[49]

Rivalries within the party occasionally even led to the suppression of works that did not deviate greatly from the Orthodox line. One victim of such suppression was the work of Ts'ao Ya-po, *Wu-ch'ang ko-ming chen-shih* (The true story of the Wuchang Revolution) [232]. In this three-volume work, Ts'ao attempted to demonstrate the importance of the Hupeh groups in revolutionary history, particularly with regard to the role played by those Hupeh secret societies with which he had been affiliated. He managed not only to offend the revolutionaries from Kwangtung and other provinces but even to antagonize those Hupeh revolutionaries who did not belong to his group; and it was this that led to the suppression of his work.[50] Sympathy for the author has led to an exaggeration of the actual merit of his account. Although the book has long been superseded by more comprehensive and meticulous efforts by other Hupeh revolutionaries (these works are discussed in the next section[51]), it nevertheless has value as the first major work to treat the Wuchang Uprising as the center of events.

## THE EVOLUTION OF
## HISTORICAL WRITING, 1937-49

During the 1937-49 period historical study of the Revolution, by avoiding direct challenge to Orthodox canons, developed slowly but steadily in the direction of broadening the scope of investigation and of more systematic accumulation and codification of data. This development was made possible by certain political and ideological changes that occurred in the years following the outbreak in 1937 of the second Sino-Japanese War.

First, in the face of mounting nationalistic sentiment against Japanese aggression, the role played by the Japanese in the history of the Revolution became increasingly embarrassing. Since it was impossible to deny the intimate association of the Japanese with Sun Yat-sen and with other revolutionaries, the only alternative was to shelve, in the Orthodox version, a considerable portion of Sun's revolutionary career.

Second, by leading the fight against the Japanese, the Nationalists acquired a much broader basis for national leadership than they had commanded in the previous decade, when they had based their claim to rule primarily on the theory that they were continuing to carry out the National Revolution. In consequence, revolutionary history became less important as a political tool.

Third, during the war period party historians began to glorify the Northern Expedition at the expense of earlier revolutionary history because it was during the Northern Expedition that the wartime leaders had risen to power. The revolutionary history was thus farther removed from the realm of current politics, and the historians had relatively more freedom in dealing with it.

Fourth, with the passage of time, the revolutionary élan of the Nationalists lost momentum; and although they had no intention of giving up their monopoly of the interpretation of the Revolution, much of their early enthusiasm for identifying themselves with the revolutionary forerunners had been dissipated.

For these reasons, revolutionary history receded into the background of the political scene. There followed a gradual relaxation of official interference, and the historiography on the Revolution was able to strike out in new directions. The relaxation of Orthodox domination was first reflected in the publication of many biographical works giving some positive evaluation to public figures who had been dismissed by the Nationalists as anti-revolutionary. Some of the personalities who had played an active role during the Revolution had been simply "de-personized" during the decade of Orthodox domination.

Now there appeared such works as *San-shui Liang Yen-sun hsien-sheng nien-p'u* (A *nien-p'u* of Liang Shih-i) [80], which stresses the role Liang Shih-i played, as the right-hand man of Yüan Shih-k'ai, in engineering the Manchu abdication.

Liang Ch'i-ch'ao is another example. During the war period some historians began to suggest that Liang's role in history was not totally negative,[52] even though he had opposed the Tung Meng Hui group. This opinion clearly won official approval in the 1940s, when the Kuo Shih Kuan, a government organ responsible for the compilation of the official "national history" (*kuo-shih*), published a biographical account of Liang in its *Kuo Shih Kuan kuan-k'an* (Bulletin of the Kuo Shih Kuan, hereafter *KSKKK*).[53] Although the author expressed reservations about Liang's political role, he admitted that Liang's writings had tremendous influence on revolutionary thought in the late Ch'ing period. The *KSKKK* published also the biographies of constitutionalist leaders such as Chang Ch'ien and T'ang Shou-ch'ien, and of T'ang Shao-i, the chief representative of Yüan Shih-k'ai in the negotiations with the revolutionaries in 1911-12. Their contributions to the founding of the Republic are recognized in the biographies.[54]

In the postwar period, many traditional historians began to express their regret at the suppression of the *Ch'ing-shih-kao* in 1927 and even petitioned for permission to republish the book with the promise that the erroneous and heretic accounts, especially those containing slights against the revolutionaries, would be corrected. Although the Nationalist ban on the book was never formally lifted, articles containing favorable remarks on it were allowed to appear even in the *KSKKK*.[55]

Another indication of the relaxing of Orthodox control was the publication of more objective accounts of the revolutionary movements and organizations which, as depicted in the Orthodox version, had stood outside of the mainstream. The authors of these accounts usually avoided challenging the Orthodox interpretation but rather concentrated their attention on facts that had been neglected or distorted. One example is

Li Hsi-pin's article entitled "Ch'ing-mo Chih-na an-sha-t'uan chi-shih" (A factual account of the China Assassination Corps in the late Ch'ing period), which gives the origin and activities of the China Assassination Corps, an anarchist group independent of the Tung Meng Hui. Until the publication of Li's first-hand information in the late 1940s, the story of this secret organization had been shrouded in mystery, and Orthodox historians had vaguely referred to it as a branch of the Tung Meng Hui.[56]

By the end of 1947 there appeared an article in *KSKKK* by Liu Ch'eng-yü entitled "Hsien-tsung-li chiu-teh lu" (Reminiscences about the virtues of the late party director [Sun Yat-sen]), which gave valuable information on the development of the Hsing Chung Hui.[57] Although Sun Yat-sen, according to Lui, was working for the overthrow of the Manchu dynasty, the "Father of the Republic" did not oppose the idea of monarchical rule until the formation in 1895 of the Hong Kong chapter of the Hsing Chung Hui. Rather, it was Yang Ch'ü-yün who forced Sun to include explicitly, in the oath that every member of the Hong Kong chapter was required to sign, the ideal of establishing a republican government. This ideal distinguished the Hsing Chung Hui from other secret societies, which at that time were still confined to the tradition of anti-dynastic rebellion. Because Yang had competed with Sun for the leadership of the early revolutionary movement, the Orthodox writers usually played down Yang's contribution to the movement. Besides, the Orthodox school could hardly accept the fact that Sun did not until 1895 include in his revolutionary program the establishment of a republican government. But Liu maintained that Sun personally had told him this story. Liu's information not only sheds new light on Yang's role in the revolutionary movement but also explains why the ideal of a republican state was not included in the program of the Honolulu chapter of the Hsing Chung Hui, which had been founded only three months earlier than the Hong Kong chapter.

Of the works suggesting a new view of the revolutionary movement, the most notable is Chang Nan-hsien's *Hu-pei ko-ming chih-chih lu* (What we know about the Revolution in Hupeh), which is a carefully selected collection of documents, as well as historical writings by various authors, covering a wide range of revolutionary activities in the mid-Yangtze valley [17]. The main part of the book consists of over seventy biographies of re-volutionaries who were mostly from Hupeh but not always Tung Meng Hui members. Among the accounts of the earliest re-volutionary martyrs was the biography of T'ang Ts'ai-ch'ang, a member of K'ang Yu-wei's group, who launched the abortive revolt in Hankow in 1900.

In order to protect his book from attack from Orthodox quarters, Chang had not only cautiously revised the work four times before its publication in 1945, but also paid explicit homage to Sun Yat-sen's revolutionary career and recognized the leading role played in the Wuchang Uprising by members of the Tung Meng Hui's so-called Central China Branch. However, Chang stressed the autonomous character of the Central China Branch, which since its formation in Shanghai in 1910 had been completely independent of the leadership of Sun and other top-ranking members of the Tung Meng Hui who were refugees in Hong Kong or overseas. Furthermore, he pointed out that on the local scene it was the lower echelons of the revolutionary organization that had staged the Uprising. After the secret network had been discovered by the Manchu government a few days before the outbreak of the Uprising, the members in the New Army had acted on their own initia-tive while their leaders were either under arrest or in hiding.

Judging from the research possibilities suggested by Chang in a brief essay appended to the book,[58] we may conclude that his view on the Revolution appears to have been much more sophisticated than his treatment implies. One question his essay raises is how the initial Uprising could have been success-fully carried out in Wuchang, the administrative and political center of the mid-Yangtze valley, which Sun and many other revolutionaries had considered one of the most unsuitable areas for such an attempt. Another question is how this great historic act could have been staged spontaneously by the soldiers. He pointed out that although many students took part in the Uprising, the main revolutionary force in 1911-12 in Hupeh was made up of soldiers.

In contrast to the usual charge of opportunism leveled against the gentry leaders for their radical shift from support of the movement for a constitutional monarchy to cooperation with the revolutionaries, Chang points to the idealistic element prevailing among the gentry leaders, at least in Wuchang, during the Uprising. For instance, while Li Yüan-hung was unwilling to become governor of Wuchang, neither the revolutionaries nor the constitutionalist gentry attempted to seize that post. Chang left these and other questions unanswered, but he certainly had them in mind when he was selecting materials for the book.

Chang's book also marks the culmination of another substantial development during the period, namely, the compilation of primary materials and reminiscences by surviving participants. In contrast to the works produced during the preceding period by such revolutionist-historians as Tsou and Feng, these compilers usually avoid the presumption of addressing their works as histories, but prefer rather to regard them as source materials for the use of professional historians. Although many of the characteristic defects that we have pointed out in Feng Tzu-yu's work may be found also in these writings, the accounts they render generally manifest a higher degree of accuracy than the ''histories'' of the preceding period. Where personal reminiscences are given, the authors tend to restrict themselves to the presentation of first-hand information. The more serious works among them, such as Chang's book, both set a standard and serve as a stimulus for future writings of the surviving participants.

A third feature of the expansion of the scope of investigation was a shift from the heavy concentration of writings on Sun Yat-sen's career and on the movement in Kwangtung to a much broader coverage of revolutionary activities in other regions. Above all, a great number of writings was produced by the surviving revolutionaries from Hupeh. For example, among the authors of the more valuable works, Chang Yü-k'un [22], Chü Cheng,[59] Li Lien-fang,[60] Hu O-kung,[61] and Hu Tsu-shun[62] were all revolutionaries from Hupeh. Chang Nan-hsien, whose work has already been discussed, was also from Hupeh. This shift from an emphasis on Kwangtung was in part a reflection of the shift of power among regional groups within the party. On the one hand, after Hu Han-min's death in 1936 and Wang Ching-wei's defection to the Japanese side in 1938, the Cantonese were unable to recapture the prestige they had enjoyed before the outbreak of the war. On the other hand, after the central government was moved first to Wuhan, then to Chungking, the influence of groups from Hupeh, Szechwan, and the southwestern provinces increased rapidly.

Much more significant than the political factors, however, was the growth of a genuine interest in the Revolution as a historical subject. This interest led to a gradual expansion of the scope of investigation, far beyond the scope that Sun's career could cover. Thus, besides the writings by Hupeh revolutionaries, a number of works on the revolutionary movement in Szechwan [48], Hunan [115], Kiangsi,[63] Shanghai,[64] and even about the Luan-chou Uprising in North China [87], were produced during the war and postwar periods, even though in these periods financial support for such publications was far more difficult to obtain than in the prewar decade.

There was also the tendency among Orthodox historians to substantiate their interpretations by using more reliable sources and by applying systematic methods in their writings. One example of this development is Tsou Lu's effort to revise and enlarge his *Draft History*.[65] Feng Tzu-yu, too, became more productive and more serious during this period. In addition to completing the later volumes of the aforementioned *History*[66] and a few shorter writings [83], [84], Feng started another major enterprise, the publication of the *Ko-ming i-shih* (Anecdotes of the Revolution).[67] While the writings compiled under this title could have developed into a collection of random notes and gossip, much of the work turned out to be valuable source material for historians.[68]

More systematic works of the Orthodox school were produced by the younger generation of historians. For example, after the party authorities received from the British the original records relating to Sun's education at a medical school in Hong Kong, they assigned to Lo Hsiang-lin, who had received formal training in historical study at Tsing Hua University, the task of investigating these documents. The result was *Kuo-fu chih ta-hsüeh shih-tai* (The college life of Sun Yat-sen), which remains a definitive study on the subject [180].

Hsü Shih-shen's annotation to Sun's autobiography [109] represents a different type of Orthodox writing. Not aiming at the discovery of new facts or the presentation of new documents, the work substantiates Sun's account of the revolutionary movement by giving detailed documentation from primary sources to *every* sentence of the autobiography.

In addition to these individual works of the Orthodox school of the period, the Nationalist Party also assumed more central leadership through a Committee for the Compilation of Party History. Inaugurated as early as 1930,[69] the committee accumulated in the subsequent decades a sizeable collection of primary documents as well as manuscripts and oral accounts rendered by surviving revolutionists. While some of the materials compiled under its sponsorship were published in the 1930s and 1940s,[70] the significance of the committee's work was not fully recognized until after the committee, with its archives, had moved to Taiwan in 1949 and had begun during the 1950s and 1960s to publish gigantic series on the Revolution.[71]

In order to deny its puppet character under Japanese control, Wang Ching-wei's regime in Nanking also claimed the mantle of Sun Yat-sen, and consequently placed a still greater emphasis on the Orthodox interpretation of the Revolution. During the difficult years of war, however, Wang's group produced very few significant works,[72] except for the embellished accounts, with detailed documentation, of Wang's heroic attempt in 1910 on the Manchu prince-regent [7], [6].

To sum up this chapter, following the Northern Expedition the Orthodox interpretations advanced by the Nationalists began to dominate historical writings on the Revolution. There emerged several important works of the Orthodox school during the 1927-37 decade; but so far as historical thinking is concerned, these works contributed little beyond the scope originally set by Sun Yat-sen and his close associates. In the meantime, the Nationalists had succeeded in suppressing the publication of heretical writings on the Revolution. Historical study during this decade was further limited by two conditions. First, professional historians tended to avoid the touchy subject of the Revolution, while enthusiastic revolutionary historians lacked the training and skill for monographical writings. Second, regional and clique politics seriously restricted historical interpretation even within the Orthodox framework.

The national crises that were precipitated by the Sino-Japanese war in 1937 removed the history of the Revolution from the forefront of the political scene and made possible a more detached appraisal of the Revolution and a differentiation between its history and the political ideology and political myths surrounding it. Thus, the period 1937-49 witnessed a slow but steady development of historical writings on the subject. Among these there appeared, for instance, the more objective accounts of Liang Ch'i-chao and others who had stood outside the revolutionary camp. There emerged also writings on those revolutionary personalities and movements whose significance had been played down in the Orthodox version. In the meantime, the Orthodox school itself also showed signs of more historical discipline. Moreover, the large number of personal accounts rendered by surviving participants not only provided valuable sources for historical study but also set the momentum for the production of autobiographical works to be continued on the Chinese mainland and in Taiwan after 1949.

However, all of these developments occurred within the

general doctrinal framework of the Orthodox school. Despite the tendency toward more scholarly writing, the historians of the thirties and forties avoided almost entirely any frontal assault on the Orthodox canons. The long-continued domination of the official school not only resulted in a well elaborated Orthodox version but also produced an inertia in historical thinking, both of which continued to affect the study of the Revolution even after 1949 when the political conditions that had given rise to the Orthodox views ceased to exist.

# — 4 —

# Neo-Orthodox Domination
# since 1949

Since the takeover in 1949, Communist interpretations on the Revolution have been exalted to the dominant position previously enjoyed by the Orthodox school. In order to provide a proper perspective, our survey begins with a summary of the pre-1949 Communist writings on the Revolution, which are limited in total quantity but which already contain some of the features of the post-1949 Neo-Orthodox writings. There follows an examination of the major historical compilations since 1949, by far the most important product of the school for the use of scholars outside Communist China. Finally, we turn to an examination of the school's intrinsic tensions and problems as manifested in the representative writings.

## EARLY COMMUNIST VIEWS
## ON THE REVOLUTION, 1923-49

During their revolutionary days in the twenties and thirties, many Communist writers pointed to the Revolution as a lesson for their own movement. Although few of them had the inclination to study seriously the Revolution itself, their discussions already contained many of the features predominant today in the trend of historiography on the Chinese mainland.

It was during the period of the Nationalist-Communist alliance in the mid-twenties that the party organ, *Hsiang-tao chou-pao* (the Guide Weekly) [300] and other Communist journals began to put forth discussions on the Revolution as part of their effort to assess the revolutionary role of Sun Yat-sen and his party. With the usual enthusiasm of new converts, the Chinese Communists were eager to apply to China their recently learned Marxist-Leninist docrines, especially the Leninist theory of revolution in colonial countries. Accordingly, they interpreted the Revolution as both a national and a bourgeois-democratic revolution. Their observations of these two aspects of the Revolution may be summed up in two of their slogans: "anti-feudal" *(fan feng-chien)* and "anti-imperialist" *(fan-ti)*, both of which were to be echoed again and again in Communist writings during the ensuing decades.

These early Communist interpretations may be traced to Ch'en Tu-hsiu's articles in 1923. Ch'en maintained that the revolutionists and the constitutionalists, both representing bourgeois elements in the Chinese society of the late Ch'ing, differed from each other only in the means by which they sought to attain their ultimate goal, not in the goal itself, which was to renovate and strengthen China. This kind of goal, as Ch'en stressed, was "universal to all the bourgeois-democratic movements of the colonial and semi-colonial countries."[73]

As a bourgeois-democratic revolution, however, Ch'en regarded the 1911-12 experience as a complete failure—a failure that he attributed mainly to the weakness of the bourgeoisie as a class that "had not completely differentiated itself from the official-feudal class and had not grown to a degree that a class consciousness could emerge and a need for revolution be felt."[74] Consequently, he contended, the radical elements of the bourgeoisie, as represented by Sun's group, succeeded only in knocking out the Manchu throne, which was nothing more than a symbol of feudal rule. But the Revolution itself was defeated in China by overwhelming feudal forces.

If Ch'en's arguments gave the impression that his emphasis was on the "anti-feudal" theme and that he did not put sufficient stress on the Leninist doctrine on the role of imperialism in the Chinese Revolution, this official line was soon fully spelled out by P'eng Shu-chih in his article celebrating the thirteenth anniversary of the Wuchang Uprising.[75] The Revolution, according to P'eng's analysis, was a result chiefly of the long-continued impact of Western capitalism upon China's feudal economy. He maintained that capitalist imperialism destroyed the traditional economy of small production and created a class of *Lumpenproletariat;* that Western capitalism also brought forth a new commercial bourgeoisie and aroused among them a desire for building up industry self-owned and independent of foreign influence; that capitalism caused the deterioration of the feudal landlord class; and that it deepened the antagonisms between the landlord class and the new bourgeoisie until, finally, the bourgeoisie and its representative, the new intelligentsia, came to be aware of the oppressive and exploiting nature of imperialism. In the perspective of this developmental process he saw imperialist aggression as both "ultimate cause" and "chief enemy" of the revolutionary movement. Unfortunately, P'eng lamented, by 1911 the aggressive feature of imperialism had not yet been fully recognized in China; and the revolutionary regime was soon played into the hands of the imperialist running dog, Yüan Shih-k'ai.

Such anti-imperialist cries as voiced by P'eng, however, did not lead the communist writers to any serious investigation of foreign responses to the Revolution. Nor was much attention paid to the fact that imperialism was less aggressive in the China of 1911 than it had been in the last decade of the nineteenth century. Thus, early Communist writings suggest on the whole a crude, dogmatic (though undoubtedly enthusiastic) application of the Marxist-Leninist doctrine to what was considered a national bourgeois revolution.

Nevertheless the spirit underlying this simple and crude application of the Leninist doctrine is meaningful. It was in the wake of the Bolshevik Revolution that Marxism first thrust itself upon the attention of Chinese intellectuals. Although Chu Chih-hsin had introduced Marx and the *Communist Manifesto*

in the *Min Pao* as early as 1906,[76] Marxism did not capture
the imagination of Chinese intellectuals until after 1917, when
news of events in Russia seemed to confirm the Marxist
prophecy of a world revolution or, more fundamentally, of a
redemptive historical process that would lead, for China, to
eventual transformation and salvation. This faith in the infallible predictability of the Marxist-Leninist doctrines still
underlies and animates Communist discussions on the Revolution, though in more recent decades communist views, as we
shall discuss later, have been complicated by other considera-
tions.

Following the fast-moving events of the Northern Expedition in 1926-28, the Communists were forced again and again
to justify their positions vis-à-vis the Nationalists. As a result,
Ch'ü Ch'iu-pai, Li Li-san, and others produced many polemical treatises on the development of the revolutionary situation
in China. So far as the Revolution of 1911 is concerned, however, the voluminous arguments over the relationship of class
forces during 1911-12 contained nothing original. For instance,
the attacks launched against P'eng Shu-chih's social analysis
[199] by Ch'ü Ch'iu-pai are well known; but so far as the Revolution is concerned, Ch'ü's interpretations are not substantially
different from P'eng's."

To such dogmatic writings there is one brilliant exception:
Kuo Mo-jo's autobiographical piece, *Fan-cheng ch'ien-hou*
(Around the Revolution [of 1911]).[78] With a light touch of the
Marxist-Leninist interpretation, but with a novelist's gift for
observation, Kuo renders a readable and convincing account of
the actual happenings in Szechwan during the 1911-12 period.
He depicts the influence of the constitutionalist leaders; the
arrogance, the naïveté and, later, the corruption of the revolutionist rulers; and the dreams and fears among the student-
intelligentsia of his generation. Above all, his vivid recollections of
the mass petitioning and mass slaughter that followed the disputes
over the "railway issue," on the eve of the Revolution, make this

work a valuable historical document.

After the breakup of their alliance with the Nationalists in 1927, when many Communists began to reflect seriously on their own experiences during these eventful years, several monographs on the "Great Revolution of 1925-27" were produced. Among the writings that discussed the 1911 Revolution as a historical background for the 1925-27 drama was a book by Chu Hsin-fan (also known as Chu Ch'i-hua) entitled *Chung-kuo ko-ming yü Chung-kuo she-hui ko chieh-chi* (The Chinese revolution and the social classes in China) [50]. Chu followed the Marxist-Leninist line of interpretation, but unlike other Communist writers of the period he paid some attention to documentation and to factual detail. While his account of the 1911 Revolution suggests some Orthodox influence, especially that of Tsou Lu's *Draft History,* he maintained that the Hsing Chung Hui movement went through a process of transformation from reformism to revolution. If we may judge from the obscure purpose of Hsing Chung Hui's initial pronouncements as well as from the reformist zeal in Sun's *Memorial* to Li Hung-chang, the nature of the Hsing Chung Hui at its incipient stage seems to Chu to have been very close to the "national self-strengthening" movement. Although this view was shelved by the prevailing Orthodox school, it was to be raised again in later Communist writings.

Another well-known work, *I-chiu erh-wu chih i-chiu erh-ch'i ti Chung-kuo ta-ko-ming-shih* (The great revolution in China: 1925-27), by Hua Kang [123], also contains some account of the Revolution. Hua Kang called attention to the late Ch'ing campaign "for wresting mining and railway construction rights from foreign control." Although he made little attempt to explore research possibilities in this direction, the mining-and-railway issue he raised was to be used by Communist writers to illustrate their "economic history"-oriented and anti-imperialist interpretations. If one may judge from its quality, the book would not have enjoyed such fame as it did had not the Nationalist government banned it immediately after its publication in 1931 and imprisoned its author for about seven years. In the early thirties the book continued to circulate clandestinely under different covers and to find popular acceptance in radical youth circles.[79]

In 1938, after the Communists had joined the Nationalists in a united front to oppose the Japanese invasion, Hua Kang emerged from jail a popular leftist writer. But he found, like Rip Van Winkle returning to his village after a long sleep, that public sentiment and the issues of the day had completely changed. Now, in the face of the massive military invasion by the Japanese, there was no need for theoretical argument to convince the Chinese public of the evil influence of imperialism on Chinese social and economic development. The simple and direct xenophobic cry brought a welcome emotional release. Hua Kang thus revised and enlarged his book, in which the new emphasis was placed upon China's suffering at foreign hands rather than upon China's backwardness in contrast with Western civilization. The themes of national survival and national independence are clearly implied in the title of the revised version, *Chung-hua min-tsu chieh-fang yün-tung shih* (A history of the Chinese people's liberation movement) [122]. The problem of anti-feudal class struggle, though still regarded as important, was no longer their chief concern.

The revision of Hua Kang's work, of course, had as its immediate political purpose popular appeal. But more significantly, it also evidenced an important shift of basic value orientation in leftist writing on Chinese history. It was a shift from "universalistic faith" in Marxism-Leninism as a sovereign key for the explanation of human history (of which Chinese history was but one part) to a new, "particularistic" reverence for and interest in China's past. For many leftist writers this reorientation, at first enunciated rather inauspiciously, was to point to a new concept of national destiny.

In the survey of early Communist writings on the Revolution, we have pointed out the universalistic faith that underlay the dogmatic application of Marxist-Leninist doctrines to the writing of the history of the Revolution. With this faith, it was natural for Communist writers to feel an urgent need to master such conceptual schemes as "feudalism" and "bourgeois revolution," a need often too pressing to allow them to divert much attention to past happenings. Consequently, many Communist writings of the twenties and thirties indicate a greater familiarity on the part of the writer with Marxist-Leninist tenets than with Chinese history.

Following the outbreak of the Sino-Japanese war, however, mounting nationalistic sentiment favored the creation of a particularistic history for China—a history that would present China and her past as unique. Suddenly, to acknowledge this uniqueness was to invite respect among Communist and non-Communist intellectuals alike. Further, the fact that in their effort to attract popular support Communist politicians had also to pay attention to this growing sentiment in turn affected profoundly the psychology of the Communist leadership. To be sure, Marxist-Leninist canons were still sacred to them, and China was still categorized as a semi-colonial and semi-feudal country for which a national, bourgeois-democratic revolution was required. But beneath the "anti-feudal" and "anti-imperialist" cries of the time there was discernible a mounting interest in the indigenous culture and history of China.[80]

A detailed discussion of the general intellectual trends of the Chinese Communist movement is beyond the scope of this study. Nevertheless, it is clear in the wartime historical writings that much more attention was now being paid to what the Chinese people were able to accomplish than to why they had failed to achieve the standards set by Western civilization. By highlighting positive accomplishments, Communist writers now tended to give a higher rating to the 1911 Revolution as well as to other events in recent history. Above all, the writings of Mao Tse-tung and many other Communist leaders suggest a growing belief that China's unique and original historical development constitutes a major contribution to human heritage.

So far as the view of the Revolution itself is concerned, the most important development was the thesis advanced by Mao Tse-tung concerning the "old" and the "new" democratic revolutions.[81] While the Chinese Revolution still has to pass through the "bourgeois-democratic" and the "socialist" stages, the first stage, according to Mao, is to be further divided into two sub-stages: (1) the "old-democratic" revolution, which culminated in the 1911 Revolution and was led by the bourgeoisie; and (2) the "new-democratic" revolution, which is now led by the proletariat or its emanation, the Communist Party. The first stage, according to Mao, began with the Opium War in 1840, i.e., when China's feudal society started changing into a semi-colonial and semi-feudal one, and all of modern Chinese history since the Opium War, according to his thesis, may be regarded as a manifestation of the revolutionary process. "In a fuller sense," Mao writes, however, "it was the Revolution of 1911 which marked the outbreak of the 'old-democratic' revolution in China." He maintains that owing to the restrictions of historical conditions, the "old-democratic" revolution is not yet completed; that the historical significance of the 1911 Revolution should nonetheless be noted; that its goals were correct; and furthermore, that its unaccomplished missions are to be carried out by the "new-democratic" revolution under the leadership of the Communists. Although the focus of Mao's attention was upon "new-democratic" revolution, it is the historical role he assigned to the 1911 Revolution that has become the point of departure for Neo-Orthodox discussions on the subject.

Mao's effort to link the unfulfilled mission of the Revolution with the "new-democratic" revolution certainly reflects Communist strategy under the wartime United Front policy. In order to compete with the Nationalists for popular support, the Communists claimed the mantle of Sun Yat-sen, and even argued that the Communist movement at the time of the Japanese invasion was closer to the true spirit of Sun's Three Principles than was the Nationalist. Thus, instead of challenging the Orthodox version of the Revolution, they took advantage of Orthodox myths to exploit the popular image of Sun.

There are available some wartime textbooks on modern

Chinese history produced in Yenan that expound the party line of the period.[82] In addition, many articles presenting Communist views on the Revolution may be found in the *Chieh-fang jih-pao* (Liberation Daily), a leading newspaper in Yenan, where October 10, the anniversary of the Wuchang Uprising in 1911, was observed annually as National Independence Day. Among the commemorative articles are historical essays by Fan Wen-lan and others, elaborating on the Maoist interpretations, as well as reminiscent writings by such Communist leaders as Chu Teh and Lin Po-ch'ü, who had participated in the Revolution. [83]

In the course of their intensified struggles against the Nationalists during the last years of the war and in the postwar period, the Communists also drew heavily upon their investigations into Chinese history for immediate political purposes. A particularly popular work was Ch'en Po-ta's *Ch'ieh-kuo ta-tao Yüan Shih-k'ai* (The great usurper Yüan Shih-k'ai), in which the usurper of the revolutionary government was portrayed in such a way as to suggest Chiang Kai-shek's rule [32], [33], [79]. This work, published first in 1945 in *Ch'ün-chung* (The Masses), a Communist journal in Chungking, and later in book form, was a propaganda success. A few years later a young Communist historian, Li Nai-han (better known today as Li Shu), followed Ch'en's example and treated the Revolution in a broader fashion in his *Hsin-hai ko-ming yü Yüan Shih-k'ai* (The revolution of 1911 and Yüan Shih-k'ai) [164].

Another major propaganda work based on historical study was Hu Sheng's *Ti-kuo-chu-i yü Chung-kuo cheng-chih* (Imperialism and Chinese politics) [119]. To assail the popular image of the United States, which was giving financial and military aid to the Nationalist regime in the civil war of the 1940s, Hu Sheng dug up evidence of the disastrous effects of foreign intervention in Chinese politics during the Revolution of 1911 as well as during other major crises of modern history.

Hu Sheng also wrote in booklet form for the Communist-sponsored series *Wan-jen ts'ung-shu*, or *Ten Thousand People's*

*Library*, a succinct account of Sun Yat-sen's revolutionary career, in which he pointed out some errors in the prevalent Orthodox version of Sun's career [118].

Such pre-1949 Communist writings relating to the Revolution add up to only a small number; yet in them are already present many features of the Neo-Orthodox school: the "anti-feudal" and "anti-imperialist" slogans, the application of Marxist-Leninist canons, the Maoist interpretations, the use of revolutionary history for propaganda purposes, and the strategy to exploit rather than to challenge the prevalent Orthodox version, including the popular image of Sun. Above all, the origin of the basic incompatibility of the particularistic and universalistic orientations may be traced to the wartime Communist writings.

## MAJOR DOCUMENTARY
## COMPILATIONS, 1950-66

The Chinese Marxist historians thus had developed an activist tradition of using history as a vehicle for political struggle long before 1949. Moreover, like many dynastic founders in Chinese history, the new Peking rulers have been eager to see the historical records presented according to, and in support of, their "correct" view of history.[84] As a result, the compilation and publication of vast quantities of documents and source materials on the Revolution have formed the most impressive feature of Neo-Orthodox historiography.

As early as October, 1949, the Communist leadership began to explore the possibility of compiling a series of topics on modern history. The result was the huge collection entitled *Chung-kuo chin-tai-shih tzu-liao ts'ung-k'an* (Collections of source materials on modern Chinese history),[85] of which the ninth collection was entitled *Hsin-hai ko-ming* (The Revolution of 1911, hereafter *HHKM*) [2]. It took more than six years for seven editor-compilers to complete this eight-volume compendium of *HHKM*, a task in which the assistance of established scholars was solicited. Documents and reminiscent writings are grouped according to major topics, which are generally arranged in chronological order and reflect the major interests of the Neo-Orthodox school: the pioneering revolutionary groups, the early attempts at military uprising, the Tung Meng Hui organization and its activities, the peasant disturbances, the railway disputes, the Wuchang Uprising, the revolutions in provinces, the establishment of the Provisional Government in Nanking, the intervention of imperialist powers, etc. Appended to the last volume are two well-selected and annotated bibliographies compiled by Ch'ai Te-keng and Chang Tz'u-ch'i. In cases where certain items are too long to be included in full, the criteria for omission are often justifiable. Typographical errors in the original sources have been corrected or pointed out. For writings espousing an anti-revolutionary viewpoint, brief Neo-Orthodox editorial comments are given, but the original text is unaltered. The publication of the *HHKM* sets a new standard in China for historical compilations on the Revolution.

Another splendid collection entitled *Hsin-hai ko-ming ch'ien shih-nien-chien shih-lun hsüan-chi* (Selections of writings on current affairs during the decade preceding the Revolution of 1911) is projected to include in six volumes all the leading articles in the available journals of the 1901-10 period, as well as selections from some influential revolutionary books. Four volumes, covering articles up to 1907, have been published. If we may judge from the materials in these volumes, most of which had been almost inaccessible, this collection is a must for students of the intellectual history of early twentieth-century China [16].

Following these examples, several collections have been published on the revolutionary activities in various provinces[86] and on the railway disputes in Szechwan [222]; the original texts of revolutionary journals, such as the complete set of *Min Pao*, were photoreproduced [322]; the periodical *Chin-tai-shih tzu-liao* (Materials on modern history), which was founded in 1954 to publish rare materials [292], devoted its twenty-fifth issue to sources on the Revolution [65]. Besides, several recent compilations on modern history include also important materials on the revolutionary movement.[87] A list of such documentary reproductions could be endless.

Another type of compilation on the Revolution is the collaborative effort to render reminiscent accounts by survivors of 1911. The Neo-Orthodox themes are usually stressed at the beginning and end of each account, and an introductory essay is sometimes supplied to provide the "correct" interpretation. In the narration, however, the primary attention of the writer has been directed to actual happenings in the past rather than to their ideological relevance to the present.

The most impressive enterprise of this kind is the *Hsin-hai ko-ming hui-i-lu* (Recollections on the Revolution of 1911), the first five volumes of which have appeared. They contain two hundred seventy-six memoirs recently written, individually or collaboratively, by participants or eyewitnesses of the Revolution [63]. In similar fashion participants in the Wuchang Uprising produced their accounts in about five hundred thousand words, a portion of which is included in the volumes entitled *Hsin-hai shou-i hui-i-lu* (Recollections on the first uprising in 1911) [64]. Since many of these accounts were rendered by New Army soldiers who had staged the Uprising, these memories provide an indispensable source for the study of the military aspect of the Revolution.

Among the autobiographical works containing first-hand information, the writings of Ho Hsiang-ning [94], Wu Yü-chang [268], and other prominent figures in the People's Republic are widely read in China and abroad. A work of greater interest to us is the autobiography of Henri Pu Yi, the last emperor of the Manchu dynasty, entitled *Wo ti ch'ien-pan-sheng* (The first half of my life) [1]. Pu Yi was six years old at his abdication, too young to have participated in any meaningful way in the 1911-12 events. And it is understandable that he felt it much more necessary to load his autobiography with Communist jargon than would many veteran Communists. Nevertheless, despite all these reservations his autobiography provides valuable background information on the Manchu court, which stood as the chief target of the Revolution and which may be studied both as a power group and as a political institution.

In addition to these works, a number of research guides to the study of the Revolution have been published.[89] Some bibliographies are included in Chang Ching-lu's series of *Chung-kuo chin-tai ch'u-pan shih-liao* (Source materials on the history of modern Chinese publications).[90] Ch'ien Hsing-ts'un (alias Ah Ying and Chang Yü-ying), who began to compile various bibliographies on modern China in 1934 when his leftist activities were seriously restricted under Nationalist surveillance, has produced several useful lists on the Revolution.[91] The most valuable one, which has been included in various collections and journals, is his *Hsin-hai ko-ming shu-cheng* (An annotated bibliography on the 1911 Revolution),[92] which complements and contrasts with the two above-mentioned bibliographies appended to the *HHKM* volumes. For those *HHKM* bibliographies, the criterion of selection is richness of historical information. This has resulted in a broad coverage of source materials, ranging from contemporary reports to monographical works, from the memoirs of revolutionists to accounts rendered by the Manchus. Ch'ien's work, however, is devoted to a comprehensive list of available revolutionary essays, fiction, and poetry, as well as the translations on foreign revolutionary movements produced by the revolutionists themselves or by their sympathizers in the late Ch'ing period. It is thus a unique guide to the study of the intellectual by-products of the revolutionary movement.

Generally speaking, Western scholars hold in fairly high esteem such compilations from the mainland. Many hitherto inaccessible materials are included, with the selected documents faithfully transcribed; and editorial comments advancing official doctrines are kept to a minimum. No evidence of fabrication has been found. The Neo-Orthodox interpretations certainly form a basic framework for the vigorous selection and arrangement of documents in these compendia. Nevertheless, by making the important source materials on certain issues easily available, these compilations have undoubtedly stimulated historical study on the Revolution. Though almost no significant work has come out of the mainland since the Cultural Revolution of 1966, we have reason to assume that more materials of the same high quality will be compiled and published once a climate favorable to historical compilation has been restored.

## PROBLEMS OF INTERPRETATION, 1950-66

In addition to such compilations, there was also a steady flow of scholarly publications from the Mainland in the fifties and early sixties. Aside from some books of general history,[93] the great majority of the Neo-Orthodox writings appear in the form of articles in *Li-shih yen-chiu* (Journal of historical studies, hereafter LSYC) and other historical periodicals.[94] There is also available the report or résumé of the discussions at the modern history colloquia (*t'ao-lun-hui*) held in Peking, Shanghai, and other major cities.[95] The most important activity in recent years, however, was the six-day Research Conference for the Celebration of the Jubilee of the Revolution, held in Wuhan in 1961. More than a hundred historians participated in the Conference, at which forty-six papers were presented.[96] These various bits of information suggest that Chinese historians were more active than Westerners expected. Furthermore, if one investigates beyond the surface of monotonous repetitions of Neo-Orthodox themes and focuses his attention on nuances of emphasis in the more serious writings, he can sense throughout a general undercurrent of anxiety and tension, as manifested in their Sisyphean efforts to arrange and rearrange the massive data in order to fit them into the Neo-Orthodox framework. The challenge facing the Chinese historians may be viewed basically from two angles. First, there is the usual tension arising from the gap between doctrine and reality. The early Communist writers, with the bulk of primary sources unavailable to them, could afford to be satisfied with the dogmatic application of the Marxist-Leninist doctrines. Now, with the voluminous collections of documents pouring out, it has become increasingly apparent that the official themes are either too simplistic or too arbitrary to explain the complex story of the Revolution recorded in the documents. The Neo-Orthodox historians are indeed caught in a dilemma. On the one hand, under the tradition of Chinese historiography they cannot simply ignore the newly available documents but must give some convincing interpretation of them. This traditional value is reinforced by the rationalistic aspect of Marxism, which demands rational explanations for historical data. On the other hand, to question the applicability to Chinese history of Marxist-Leninist canons is to shake the fundamental faith upon which state myth has been built.

Secondly, the difficulties of the historians are further complicated by the incompatibility of the particularistic sentiment for Chinese history and the universalistic faith in the Marxist-Leninist model. We have touched briefly upon these two trends in the discussion on wartime Communist writings (pp. 46-47). After the end of the Sino-Japanese War, and especially after the Communist victory in 1948-49, the universalistic trend gradually regained its influence. This was manifested in the application of class analyses to every and any historical study in the first decade of Communist rule, but the particularistic sentiment was never really submerged. By 1960 many writings clearly indicated the great enhancement of the particularistic sentiment, which could not be satisfied, for instance, with equating the distinct Chinese tradition of over two thousand years with the feudal society of medieval Europe. One recent manifestation of the contradictions in the two trends is the controversy over "historicist viewpoints" *(li-shih chu-i kuan-tien)* versus "class viewpoints" *(chieh-chi kuan-tien)*, which raged during the 1963-66 period in many Chinese journals.[97]

The international conference on Chinese Communist historiography held in London in 1965 also took note of this problem: "To court both cultural uniqueness and universal applicability is a task few historians savour, yet it is one that Chinese writers today are forced to perform."[98]

These basic difficulties are laid before Chinese Communist historiography as a whole. So far as the study of the Revolution is concerned, the difficulties may be illustrated by a quick survey of the Neo-Orthodox controversies over certain major issues, namely, the role of the bourgeoisie, the "anti-Manchu" issue, and the class identity of many revolutionary leaders.

In the face of impressive new evidence, the Neo-Orthodox view of the role of the bourgeoisie, in the form of a dichotomy between the national bourgeoisie and the revolutionaries on the one hand, and the comprador bourgeoisie and the reformers on the other hand, appears far too arbitrary to explain the complicated revolutionary movement. Chinese historians' awareness of the problem is reflected in an article in *LYSC* by Liu Ta-nien, entitled "Chung-kuo chin-tai-shih chu wen-t'i" (The problems of modern Chinese history),[99] in which Liu points out that the relationship between the comprador and the national bourgeoisie needs further investigation, as does the process of differentiation within the national bourgeoisie. He raises such questions as how to draw the line between revolutionaries and reformers and what are the lines of subdivision within the bourgeois revolutionaries.

In an attempt to answer such questions, Chang K'ai-yuan and Liu Wang-lin proposed a three-strata theory as a modification of the concept of a clear-cut dichotomy. They maintained that the comprador bourgeoisie, being the running dog of the imperialists, could not play any positive role in China's modern transformation and should therefore be disinguished from the reformers. On the other hand, they suggested the national bourgeoisie be further divided into three strata. While its middle and lower strata provided the main forces for the revolutionary movement, its upper stratum would never embrace the revolutionary cause even though it might take certain progressive steps, such as those manifested in the reform attempts in 1898 and in the constitutionalist movement in the 1900s.

In a paper under their joint authorship, Chang and Liu presented the above thesis at the Wuhan Conference on the Revolution. It was entitled "Ts'ung hsin-hai ko-ming k'an min-tsu tzu-ch'an chieh-chi ti hsing-ke" (The character of the national bourgeoisie as manifested in the Revolution of 1911).[100] In similar fashion, in the Conference paper entitled "Hsin-hai ko-ming ch'ien-hsi Chung-kuo tze-peng-chu-i kung-yeh yü kung-yeh tse-ch'an chieh-chi" (Capitalist industries and the industrial bourgeoisie in China on the eve of the 1911

Revolution),[101] P'eng Yü-hsin divided the industrial bourgeoisie into three strata. This three-strata approach thus seems to represent a new trend in the thinking on the subject of the national bourgeoisie.

At the discussion sessions of the Conference, however, many participants expressed reservations about this approach.[102] One question is whether the economic stratification of the national bourgeoisie corresponded to the variations in their political outlook. Theoretically, such a correspondence should be unquestioned because the political outlook, according to Marxism, always reflects economic interests. But a majority of the Conference members felt that this kind of correspondence was often unclear and that meaningful division of political "cliques" or "wings" should be based on their political stand rather than on their economic background. For example, some pointed to Chang Ch'ien's "feudalistic" political outlook, even though they accepted his economic outlook as definitely "bourgeois." Such an attitude, if fully developed, could lead to the dangerous position of the purely "historicist viewpoint," which would disregard the basic requisites of the "class viewpoint."

These discussions on the role of the bourgeoisie inevitably gave rise to many problems concerning its relationship with other classes. For instance, one question raised at the Conference was whether the constitutionalists should be identified as the representatives of the landlord class rather than of the upper stratum of the national bourgeoisie. As some participants pointed out, the latter, by definition, should not be the enemy of the bourgeois revolution; but the hostility toward the Revolution on the part of the constitutionalists in Kweichow and some other provinces was well documented. At a historical colloquium held in Peking in 1962,[103] some historians also mentioned the difficulty of identifying the constitutionalists with the bourgeoisie. They asserted that in the late Ch'ing Provincial Assembly, members from the landlord class far outnumbered those from the bourgeoisie.

More serious difficulties arose from the discussions on the relationship between the bourgeoisie and the peasantry.

According to the Neo-Orthodox theme, the former assumed the revolutionary leadership while the latter played the role of the following masses; but there remains the problem of how the leaders actually contacted, aroused, and guided the masses. Some Neo-Orthodox writers have looked upon the secret societies as the revolutionary representative of the peasant masses, and have attempted to explore the relationship between the secret-society leaders and the bourgeois revolutionaries. Many historians, however, recognized that the class composition of these societies was very heterogeneous; and before it is decided whether the societies represent mainly the interest of the peasantry or of the *Lumpenproletariat,* there will be no end to the controversies over such questions as whether the societies were "the political representative of the peasantry in alliance with the bourgeoisie" or served merely as "the link between the two classes during the Revolution."

Bypassing the issue of secret societies, Wang I-sun proposes a new thesis on the relationship of the two classes in his Conference paper, "Hsin-hai ko-ming shih-ch'i tzu-ch'an chieh-chi yü nung-ming ti kuan-hsi wen-t'i" (The relationship between the bourgeoisie and the peasantry during the period of the 1911 Revolution).[104] Wang suggests that the rise of the revolutionary tide was reflected in the bourgeois revolutionaries' growing awareness of and sympathy for the peasant condition, while the decline of the movement coincided with the increasing alienation of the bourgeoisie from the peasant masses.

Wang's thesis, however, was criticized from two angles. First, many participants pointed out that factual evidence did not support his position. In contrast to the rising revolutionary tide during the years approaching 1911, there was at the same time a growing disillusionment with mass uprisings in general and with secret-society plots in particular. More and more the revolutionaries looked to the New Army officers for help. The Wuchang Uprising was not a massive peasant uprising but a typical military coup, staged by conspirators among New Army soldiers.

The second and more severe criticism was that Wang's thesis failed to meet the basic Marxist canons. Since ideology and politics usually reflect changing social and economic conditions, the ebb and flow of revolutionary tides depend not upon the subjective concerns of the bourgeoisie but upon a deepening of the class conflict. Thus, peasant discontent, as manifested in the form of rice riots, protests against heavy taxation, and the mass demonstrations during the railway disputes were much more significant than bourgeois concern about peasant conditions.

In spite of all these difficulties related to the problems concerning the bourgeoisie, no writer has dared to raise the question whether the bourgeoisie issue was indeed essential to the Revolution, or whether the Chinese bourgeoisie as a class, in whatever sense comparable to the French bourgeoisie of 1789, played only a marginal role in 1911.

In contrast to the voluminous writings on the bourgeoisie problem, there was virtually no serious discussion of the anti-Manchu issue until the appearance in 1961 of Liu Ta-nien's article, *Hsin-hai ko-ming yü fan-Man wen-t'i* (The Revolution of 1911 and the anti-Manchu issue). For the following two reasons, however, Neo-Orthodox historians can no longer avoid this issue. In the first place, every collection of documents and every major account of the Revolution testifies to the great emotional appeal of "anti-Manchuism" during the Revolution. Secondly, with the enhancement of the particularistic trend, the overthrow of the Manchu dynasty, which marks the end of the two-thousand-year tradition of monarchical rule in China, was accepted as a great event in the experience of the Chinese people; and the Neo-Orthodox historians feel obliged to make some sort of explanation.

Liu Ta-nien now recognizes that the anti-Manchu issue is of "great historical significance" and deserves more attention than has previously been paid to it. But in the meantime Liu argues that the issue should be viewed as another manifestation of class struggle, because the racial conflict always served the interests of one or another class throughout the Ch'ing dynasty. From this angle he tries to fit the anti-Manchu issue into the Marxist scheme: from the founding of the Ch'ing dynasty to the end of the eighteenth century, the "anti-

Manchu'' campaigns were directed by the Chinese big landlords in their struggles against the Manchu regime, which was
being supported rather by Chinese small and middle-sized
landlords; during the nineteenth century, however, the racial
issue served the interest of the revolting peasants, as manifested in the anti-Manchu pronouncements of the Taipings,
the Niens, and even the Boxers; and during the Revolution of
1911 the issue was exploited by the national bourgeoisie
because the Manchu throne had become not only the symbol
of feudal rule but also the agency of imperialist exploitation
in China.

Liu's article, which was widely publicized in *LSYC, Jen-
min jih-pao* (People's daily), and other journals and collections,[105] in a sense represents a major effort to reconcile the
particularistic and the universalistic trends—the aim of reconciliation being thinly covered in Liu's own statement: ''European
history can at no stage be equated with Chinese history. Since
the Chinese bourgeois revolution has its own distinctive features and characteristics, to depict the revolution according to
any certain type of European bourgeois revolution is as
absurd as trimming one's feet to suit [other people's] shoes.
On the other hand, it is also a distortion of history to exaggerate the Chinese characteristics and to consider the 1911
Revolution not a bourgeois revolution but a so-called domestic,
racial conflict.''

Liu's reconciliation effort, however, elicited critical comments from both sides. From the left came the charge that
since a bourgeois revolution was still the central theme of the
1911 Revolution, it should therefore not be sidetracked by the
insignificant racial conflict. Moreover, the ''leftists'' used such
arguments as the following: that the anti-Manchu propaganda
of the Taiping movement represented only the opinion of a few
frustrated literati from the feudal landlord class, that the anti-
Manchuism of the Boxers was unimportant and was soon
dropped, and that the major issues involved in the railway
policy were irrelevant to the racial issue. Thus, they concluded
that the major targets of modern Chinese mass movements, including the 1911 Revolution, were always feudalism and imperial-

ism, while the anti-Manchu issue was never so important as Liu depicted it.

Still other reservations to Liu's thesis were suggested from the right. First, anti-Manchuism, though initially advanced by the bourgeois revolutionists, gave expression to the sentiment commonly shared by a great majority of the Chinese people. In the last years of Manchu rule, the racial conflict between the Manchus and the Chinese was tangible and concrete at every level of society. Thus, it would be a distortion of history to reduce the issue to a hostility stemming from the class interest of the national bourgeoisie. Secondly, even though it would be theoretically correct to assert that the ultimate goal underlying the anti-Manchu slogan was the struggle against feudalism and imperialism, few Chinese in 1911 were so sophisticated as to recognize the goal. The masses were simply attracted by the anti-Manchu slogan itself, which had a far greater appeal than the two other slogans calling for democracy and for land reform. Third, to refute the "leftist" arguments that the racial issue in modern Chinese history was of secondary importance, they pointed out that the Taipings' anti-Manchu propaganda represented not merely the writings of a few literati from the feudal class but the policy enthusiastically supported by Taiping followers.

A third area of controversy relates to the problems arising from the class identification of many revolutionary leaders, such as Huang Hsing, Chang Ping-lin, and Sung Chiao-jen. To take Chang Ping-lin's case as an example, first he spread scandals against Sun in 1908-9, then severely criticized the excessive arrogance and moral unscrupulousness of the revolutionaries during 1911-12 and even joined with some reformists to organize a party in opposition to the Kuomintang. And finally he shifted to a rightist, anti-communist position when in the twenties Sun chose the course of alliance with the Communists. His sardonic comments on Sun, after Sun's demise, were also well known. Thus, many Neo-Orthodox writers are faced with this perplexing question: how can someone as dissident as Chang be accepted as a "good" revolutionary, or as a revolutionary at all, so long as Sun is recognized as the undisputed leader of the revolutionary movement?

The problem became even more complicated when some historians dug out evidence that many of Chang's ideas were better suited than those of Sun to the role which the Neo-Orthodox school had assigned to the revolutionists. Chang was not only a leading advocate of Chinese racialism but had "a deeper and more acute awareness" of the threat of imperialism than did Sun. Chang's criticism of Western democracy also places him to the extreme left of the bourgeois revolutionists. Above all, his view on the land problem was more radical than Sun's. By 1906, Sun had been converted to Henry George's idea of the single tax to appropriate future unearned increases of land value and thus to check the enrichment of urban residents; but Chang was already advocating the ideal of "land to the tillers," with the aim of terminating the tenant system. These findings led Hu Sheng-wu and Chin Ch'ung-chi to proclaim enthusiastically that Chang was a champion of peasant interests.

In an article under their joint authorship entitled "Hsin-hai ko-ming shih-ch'i Chang Ping-lin ti cheng-chih ssu-hsiang" (The political ideas of Chang Ping-lin in the Revolution of 1911),[106] Hu and Chin admit that Chang's thinking is confused and complicated, embracing elements from both the bourgeoisie and the peasantry as well as from the feudal class; but they maintain that "the primary aspect of his thought, up to the 1911 Revolution, reflected in a larger part the interests of the peasantry and (rural) small producers." Hou Wai-lu and others, in their books on modern intellectual history, also regard Chang as a "peasant thinker" appearing on the historical scene of late Ch'ing and advocating "peasant democracy," or *nung-ming ming-chu chu-i*.[107]

Many historians, however, could hardly accept the idea that Chang represented peasant interests, especially in view of his political outlook in the 1920s. Rather they categorized him as a radical leader of the "anti-Manchu faction from the class of the middle and small landlords."[108] They point to his sharp criticism of bourgeois democracy, to his respect for many elements of "feudal civilization" in China, and in particular to his land-reform proposals, which require excessive land holdings to be *sold* rather than *confiscated*. Chang's stand was thus depicted as that of an "enlightened landlord," who was able to foresee social troubles and whose major concern was to head off peasant disturbance in advance.

Such a view is advanced in Lo Yao-chiu's articles in *Hsiamen ta-hsüeh hsüeh-pao* (Journal of Amoy University) [109] and in Ts'ai Shang-ssu's articles in *LSYC*. [110] Liu Ta-nien also points to Chang's borrowing from those anti-Manchu writings that were produced by the leaders of the big landlord class in the early Ch'ing. [111]

Still, there are other scholars, including Shao Hsüncheng, [112] who maintain that Chang was once a bourgeois revolutionist even though he later regressed to the position of a peculiar antiquarian. At the Wuhan Conference some participants doubted that Chang's thought could ever be identified, without much distortion, with the ideology of the peasantry, the bourgeoisie, or the anti-Manchu landlord class. In short, for men like Chang Ping-lin the Neo-Orthodox historians have not been able to find a satisfactory solution in Marxist terms to the problem of "class identity."

# Development of Historiography
# in Taiwan, 1945-72

Serious historical studies on the 1911 Revolution are a fairly recent phenomenon in Taiwan. The total number of new findings, therefore, has not been impressive. But the accomplishments of our Chinese colleagues on the island nonetheless deserve consideration. Several major compilations, though they contain mainly old material, have turned up some convenient reference tools. The Orthodox school in Taiwan has not only survived the great political turmoil resulting from the Communist takeover of the Chinese mainland, but in recent years it has shown substantial development. Most significant of all, there are signs in some scholarly works pointing to a greater degree of sophistication and open-mindedness in the treatment of the subject than in earlier Orthodox works. Western scholars can hardly be completely objective in treating the works of the historians in Taiwan, who are in fact a part of our intellectual and academic community and for whom we feel a strong personal sympathy. Nevertheless, I believe historians in Taiwan would welcome an honest appraisal.

## TAIWAN AND THE REVOLUTION

Following the end of World War II, Taiwan became one province of the Republic of China. Since then it has become the fashion to highlight the historical affiliation between the island and the Chinese mainland before and during the fifty years of Japanese rule. Innumerable writings have been published on topics such as Sun Yat-sen's visits to Taiwan,[113] the revolutionary martyrs,[114] and the abortive anti-Japanese plots in the wake of the 1911 Revolution, of which the more serious accounts may be found in *T'ai-wan sheng t'ung-chih kao* (A draft gazetteer of Taiwan province) [115] and in Kuo T'ing-i, *T'ai-wan shih-shih kai-shuo* (An outline history of Taiwan) [151].

Among the anti-Japanese plots in 1912-13, the Miao-li Incident seems to have had some actual contacts with the revolutionaries in southern China.[116] Its ringleader, Lo Fu-hsing, had been a Taiwanese member of the Tung Meng Hui and had participated in its activities in Southeast Asia before 1911. In his confessions, which were found among the Japanese police records, Lo made claims that after the outbreak of the Revolution on the mainland he and his comrades were dispatched by the revolutionary governor of Fukien to develop a secret network on Taiwan. He even maintained that they had support from the revolutionary government of Kwangtung. Although it is yet to be determined to what extent Lo's accounts are exaggeration — a phenomenon not uncommon in revolutionary propaganda — his confessions have been quoted by many writers as primary documents.

Besides the main sources in Japanese, *T'ai-wan ko-ming shih* (A history of the revolutionary [movement] in Taiwan) [89], written by Han Jen (a pseudonym, meaning "the Chinese"), was an original account upon which many writings concerning the Miao-li Incident and other anti-Japanese revolts are based. First published in Nanking in 1925 and possibly the earliest work of its kind in Chinese, the book was reproduced in Taiwan immediately following the end of Japanese rule.

## DOCUMENTARY COMPILATIONS

Although the Orthodox view prevailed in Taiwan as early as the 1945-49 period, it was not until the fifties that the

Orthodox school began to flourish, as manifested in the extensive publication of documentary collections comparable in size to the enterprises on the mainland. This publication boom on the Revolution in the late fifties and the sixties was made possible by certain favorable conditions. In the first place, a number of established Chinese historians chose to take refuge in Taiwan. Also moved there were the Kuomintang Party Archives, [117] which were to play a central role in documentary publications on the Revolution. In addition, political factors contributed to the publication boom on the island. The greater need for legitimacy now prompted the Nationalists to publish historical materials illustrating their continuous leadership in the national, revolutionary process. The rivalry with the Communists over the mantle of Sun Yat-sen — which was all the more intensified on the part of Nationalists after their flight to Taiwan — further stimulated them to invest funds and energy for the extensive publications on revolutionary history in general and on Sun's career in particular.

Thanks to these circumstances, several useful compendia have been produced. Since 1958 the Kuomintang Archives, for instance, have been publishing the series *Ko-ming wen-hsien* (Documents on the Revolution, hereafter *KMWH*) [73], which is designed as a documentary collection on the revolutionary movement, covering all its five "stages" according to Orthodox doctrine, i.e., from the Hsing Chung Hui period up to the present phase of "nationalist revolution" (see Ch. 1, pp. 5-8). The first five volumes of this series, which are devoted to the revolutionary movement up to 1911, contain many valuable documents on the Hsing Chung Hui and the Tung Meng Hui, especially on their organizational aspects. The hitherto unpublished autobiography of Hu Han-min is also to be found here. Another major compendium is *Ko ming jen wu chih* (Collective biographies of revolutionaries), with about 1,500 biographical sketches published in nine volumes up to 1972 [351].

To celebrate the fiftieth anniversary of the Revolution, the Nationalist leaders have undertaken a still more important compilation under the general title of *Chung-hua min-kuo k'ai-kuo wu-shih-nien wen-hsien* (A documentary collection in celebration of the Jubilee of the founding of the Republic of China, hereafter the *Jubilee Collection*) [57]. This work, twenty-one volumes of which have appeared since 1961, suggests in many respects the culmination of the development of the Orthodox school during the past half-century.

With a much more vigorous editorial effort in the selection and arrangement of documents than the *HHKM* series from the mainland, the compilers of the *Jubilee Collection* first mapped out in minute detail a framework according to Orthodox canons and then adopted from the major sources only those documents, chapters, or passages which fit into the framework. The compilers apparently intend to cover as broadly as possible, within the Orthodox framework, the materials and interpretations that have been brought forth in recent decades. For example, under the subtitle "Hsing Chung Hui" there are included many revolutionary episodes contemporaneous with but totally independent from the Hsing Chung Hui movement. Similar treatment may be found in the volumes for the Tung Meng Hui. Some of the less controversial parts of the works of early non-Orthodox authors, like Shang Ping-ho and Ku Chung-hsiu, are included as well. Among the hitherto unpublished materials, there are the manuscripts from the Kuomintang Archives, translations from Japanese police records, and the diplomatic documents in the custody of the Institute of Modern History at the Academia Sinica.

What seems to mark the major advancement of the Orthodox school is the effort in the *Jubilee Collection* to give a broad perspective to the background of the revolutionary movement. Attention is no longer confined to a description of the revolutionary movement itself. Thus, under the section title "The origin of the Revolution," two volumes are devoted to materials on anti-Manchu movements throughout the Ch'ing dynasty. Other background materials have been included in six more volumes under the section titles "Encroachment of foreign powers" and "Reforms and reactionary [measures] of the Manchu court." In the volumes covered by "Encroachment of foreign

powers," emphasis is laid on the history of Russian aggression
from the north in past centuries, which, interestingly, provides an
unexpected ground of agreement with today's official Chinese
Communist line.


## BIOGRAPHICAL WRITINGS

Aside from documentary compilation and reproduction of
earlier works, biographical writings make up a major area of
the Orthodox publications during recent decades. The fact that
a large portion of these writings is focused on Sun Yat-sen
points to the continuity of the personality cult in the Orthodox
tradition. Hundreds of reminiscent articles on Sun's activities
have been produced by those who can claim some association
or acquaintance with the "father" of the Republic.
Anthologies of such works began to emerge in 1955 on the
occasion of the ninetieth anniversary of Sun's birthday, but it
is only since 1965 that such publications have really come into
vogue as the Nationalist authorities then began to sponsor a huge
political campaign to commemorate the centenary of his birth.
A National Committee for Preparing the Centenary Celebration of
the National Father's Birth was set up for this purpose, with one of
its sub-committees devoted exclusively to the promotion of publications on Sun's career and on the revolutionary movement under
Sun's leadership. Several major anthologies were subsequently
produced.

Combing through the essays in these anthologies—the
majority of which are obviously written for political propaganda purposes—a patient student of the Revolution may
nonetheless be rewarded with finding some historical pieces of
considerable merit. For instance, in the *Kuo-fu pai-nien tan-
ch'en chi-nien lun-wen-chi* (Collected essays in commemoration of
the centenary of Sun Yat-sen's birth) [60], one may find among
other contributions a solid piece of historical work by Lo Hsiang-
lin on Sun's activities in Hong Kong.

Another example is the series of two dozen volumes, under the general title of *Kuo-fu pai-nien tan-ch'en chi-nien ts'ung-k'an* (Collective works commemorating the centenary of Sun Yat-sen's birth) produced by the Institute for the Study of the Three People's Principles. While most volumes of the collection are concerned with the interpretation or application of Sun's doctrines to current affairs, Ch'en Ku-t'ing's *Kuo-fu yü Jih-pen yu-jen* (The national father and his Japanese friends) [30] is a useful historical work, consisting of twenty-nine narratives about Sun's association with his Japanese comrades. Based mainly on Japanese sources and on the author's intimate knowledge of many Japanese participants in the revolutionary movement, this book is the first serious attempt to open up a new dimension to Chinese readers by showing the Japanese viewpoint.

Among the privately sponsored works, the most popular anthology is perhaps *Wo tsen-yang jen-shih kuo-fu Sun hsien-sheng* (How I made the acquaintance of Sun [Yat-sen]) [251], which includes not only reprints of earlier writings but also reminiscent accounts of several elder statesmen in Taiwan. These writings first appeared in *Chuan-chi wen-hsüeh* (Biographic literature) [295], a monthly journal specializing in biographical materials, and were afterward published in a collection with a subsidy from the previously mentioned National Committee.

Such writings relating to Sun's career appear also in many other journals, and it is worth noting that a number of such works have been produced by periodicals sponsored by various *t'ung-hsiang hui*, the voluntary associations organized on a provincial basis by emigrants from the Chinese mainland. To uphold the symbol of the legitimate government of all of China rather than of Taiwan island alone, the Nationalist regime has encouraged the activities of various *t'ung-hsiang hui* as one kind of trapping of the "national" government. As part of their activities, many *t'ung-hsiang hui* have sponsored their own periodicals, publishing not only documentary materials on provincial history but also nostalgic accounts by old refugees in Taiwan about the customs and the way of life in their native lands during the good old days. Many of these journals, e.g. [366], [367] and[368], seized upon the occasion of the centenary of Sun's birth to high-light the contribution of their respective native provinces to the revolutionary movement. Two good examples are *Ssu-ch'uan yü hsin-hai ko-ming* (Szechwan and the 1911 Revolution) [47] and *Kuo-fu yü Chiang-su* (Sun Yat-sen and Kiangsu) [70]. These books reproduce portions selected from other works to illuminate, respectively, the roles of the people of Szechwan and of Kiangsu in Sun's revolutionary movement.

More typical of the traditional emphasis on the edifying and exegetic functions of Chinese historians, however, are the genre called *nien-p'u*, or "biographical chronicles," in which biographic accounts and supporting documents are compiled in chronological order, with the compiler's viewpoint being revealed in his subtle presentation of information and in his very calculated choice of wording in the succinct summaries of events. The *nien-p'u* compilation has been a favorite form for Sun's biographers in Taiwan. In 1958, again the Party Archives—or more specifically the KMT Committee on Party History — published a two-volume *Kuo-fu nien-p'u [ch'u-kao]* (A [draft] *nien-p'u* of Sun Yat-sen's career, hereafter *Nien-p'u*) [74]. By setting a new standard for the writings on Sun's career in terms of clarity, comprehensiveness, and annotation of sources, the *Nien-p'u,* although spotted with many errors and imperfections, is undeniably a milestone in the development of Orthodox historiog-raphy.

Standing as a monument in a field so much charged with political sensitivity, the *Nien-p'u* has become a subject of criti-cism and dispute. The first critical review, that of Shen Yün-lung, was written rather from an academic point of view. Listing dozens of errata ranging from typographical errors to the omission of certain events as a result of dogmatic selection of facts according to Orthodox canons, Shen's review is in fact an open challenge to the Orthodox version on the Revolution.[118]

A more severe charge, however, came from within the party, when Lo Kang criticized many statements in the *Nien-p'u* from the strictly Orthodox point of view (see [183]). Lo Kang's arguments were later incorporated in his ambitious multi-volume account of Sun's career, under the title of *Chung-hua min-kuo kuo-fu shih-lu ch'u-kao* (A draft version of the veritable records of the father of the Republic of China) [182] — *shih-lu,* or "veritable records," being another form of biographical chronology, more elaborate and grandiose, usually applied to emperors. The first volume of this *Shih-lu,* covering Sun's early career and the Hsing Chung Hui period, was issued in 1965.

These and other historians may feel dissatisfied with the *Nien-p'u,* and their own works may supersede it in the future; but until such time, as Fu Ch'i-hsüeh acknowledges in his well-written *Kuo-fu Sun Chung-shan hsien-sheng chuan* (A biography of Sun Yat-sen, the father of the Republic) [88], the *Nien–p'u,* with its second revised and enlarged edition recently published [74], will remain a useful reference tool. The critical reviews of the *Nien-p'u*, however, represent an encouraging sign in a country where the book review is yet to be established as an academic tradition.

Among the biographical writings on subjects other than Sun Yat-sen, the most interesting group consists of memoirs and reminiscent accounts produced by participants in or contemporaries of the revolutionary movement. We have referred to the posthumous publications of Hu Han-min's autobiography in the above mentioned *KMWH* series. This and many other earlier publications are included in a giant-sized anthology of over a thousand pages entitled *Ko-ming hsien-lieh hsien-chin chuan* (Biographical writings of the martyrs and pioneers in the revolutionary movement) [59], which represents a fairly comprehensive coverage of the previously published biographies on those participants in the revolutionary movement whose position was acceptable to the Orthodox school. Many poems and shorter writings by these revolutionaries are appended to the biographies.While almost all of the inclusions in this anthology are reprints of earlier publications, this volume provides a very handy reference work.

Many more reminiscent accounts have been published in single volumes, in posthumous collections like those of Chang Chi [3], Chü Cheng [55], and Yen Hsi-shan [365], and in the series of *Chung-kuo hsien-tai-shih ts'ung-k'an* (Writings on modern Chinese history [259], hereafter *Ts'ung-k'an*), under the editorship of Wu Hsiang-hsiang. The previously mentioned monthly journal *Chuan-chi wen-hsüeh* also publishes important writings related to the Revolution.

The watershed of such recent development in this direction was the inauguration in 1959 of the "Oral History" project at the Academia Sinica, a project in which younger historians are engaged in assisting the older revolutionaries to record their views and experiences. In spite of many difficulties, under the guidance of Kuo T'ing-i and Hu Shih the project collected a considerable amount of information, together with original documents which these participants or observers of the Revolution had previously kept from publication. This initial success is due to certain advantages enjoyed by the project. First of all, some scholarly discipline is brought to bear on the selection and compilation of information. Second, the subjects may feel a greater sense of security and freedom in expressing their views, since the records will not be published until a date that has been fixed in accordance with their wish. In a more general sense, the "Oral History" project, by arousing an awareness of the historical significance of their experiences that would otherwise be buried forever, has in recent years also furnished the impetus for the production of serious autobiographical writings by retired statesmen and soldiers in Taiwan.


## RELAXATION
## OF ORTHODOX RESTRAINT

While all of these developments may be viewed as a continuation of the trend of historiography on the mainland during the war and the post war periods (see Ch. III, pp. 31-40), they have nevertheless gained additional momentum from some recent conditions. First, the Nationalist regime, in order to resist Communist pressures in the cold war era, was in dire need of material and moral support from the United States and other non-Communist countries. Thus it was natural for the regime to identify itself as a staunch champion of democracy facing a Communist totalitarian threat. Consequently, the Nationalists had to permit the islanders a certain political freedom, and even sponsored some experiments in democracy at the local-government level. Whatever qualifications are to be added to the observations on political progress on Taiwan, there is evidence that during the past twenty years historians and academicians have suffered comparatively less political persecution as a result of expressing their views than during the twenties and thirties.

In the second place, the cultural and intellectual influence of the United States on the island is overwhelming. Ample evidence of such influence is seen, for instance, in the growing acceptance of devices conventionally used by American scholars, such as footnotes, indices, and systematic pagination. More significantly, values such as intellectual diversity and pluralistic viewpoints have also gradually taken root in the Chinese mind, even though the need for conformity or submissiveness to the reigning Orthodoxy does not easily give way.

These favorable conditions are reflected in many historical works that could not have been published under the vigorous Orthodox domination of the 1927-37 decade. For example, the work of Ting Wen-chiang, *Liang Jen-kung hsien-sheng nien-p'u ch'ang-pien ch'u-kao* (First draft of a detailed *nien-p'u* of Liang Ch'i-ch'ao) [230], consisting of a rich collection of Liang Ch'i-ch'ao's correspondence as well as selections from his writings, is an invaluable source for the study of this great intellectual in modern Chinese history. While Liang's relatives and friends had reason for reluctance to publish the book in the middle thirties, its publication in Taipei in 1958 without many serious omissions caused no political repercussions. In this work, Liang's involvement in the constitutionalist movement is fully documented, and his debates with the advocates of the republican revolution are recorded too.

The tendency toward a more objective treatment of Liang Ch'i-ch'ao and his followers is also manifest in two historical studies. In *Liang Ch'i-ch'ao yü Ch'ing-chi ko-ming* (Liang Ch'i-ch'ao and the [late] Ch'ing revolution) [18], Chang P'eng-yüan attempts to prove that Liang's progressive writings in the late Ch'ing period definitely though inadvertently enhanced the revolutionary cause.

In 1900 Liang and many of his associates, including T'ang Ts'ai-ch'ang, were involved in the abortive Tzu-li Chün rising in Hankow, which was aimed not at a republican revolution but at restoring the throne to the reform-minded young Emperor Kuang-hsü, who had been prevented by the Empress Dowager from actually ruling. Li Shou-k'ung's scholarly investigation into the uprising was published in *Ts'ung-k'an* under the title of "T'ang Ts'ai-ch'ang yü tzu-li chün" (T'ang Ts'ai-ch'ang and the Self-reliance Army).[119]

The previously mentioned *Hsin-jen ch'un-ch'iu* [202] by Shang Ping-ho (pp. 22-23) is a work by no means acceptable to the Orthodox school, but it was reproduced in Taipei in 1962. Although the Taipei publisher was advised to withdraw the reprint from circulation after politically inspired objections had been raised, library copies are still available to scholars; and some non-controversial parts of the book, as already mentioned, are even included in the officially sponsored *Jubilee Collection*. Thus, the lenient treatment of Shang's book provides a good example of the current situation in Taiwan: while the Orthodox version is still maintained officially, the government actually takes a more tolerant attitude.

In the same direction, we see the publication of the semi-officially sponsored *Ch'ing-shih* (A history of the Ch'ing dynasty) [4], which is a revised and enlarged version of the long-banned *Ch'ing-shih-kao* [24] (see pp. 26 and 33). Those parts that contain deliberate slighting of revolutionary leaders have been omitted or rewritten, and among its appendices may be found several biographical writings on the revolutionary martyrs. A great portion of the original version, however, has been kept intact.

Although these publications generally avoid a direct confrontation with the reigning Orthodox version, they clearly manifest a growing scholarly interest in the Revolution as a historical subject. The masses of new evidence have also led historians to reconsider many widely accepted but oversimplified interpretations. The signs pointing to such reconsideration, or reinterpretation, may be found in the writings of Shen Yün-lung, whose critical review of the *Nien-p'u* of Sun Yat-sen has been mentioned above. Several of Shen's articles are included in his anthology entitled *Hsien-tai cheng-chih jen-wu shu-p'ing* (Accounts and appraisals of political figures in modern times) [205].

Generally speaking, Shen treats the Revolution as a political development with a multiplicity of contributing factors, replete with power struggles, conflicting personalities, and fortuitous events. For example, in his view, the formation of the Tung Meng Hui was not a natural outgrowth of the Hsing Chung Hui but was rather an assembly of numerous revolutionary organizations and movements. Shen points out that among the major groups which founded the Tung Meng Hui there were the Hua Hsing Hui (Society for China's Revival), headed by Huang Hsing and Sung Chiao-jen, and the Kuang Fu Hui (Society for the Restoration [of China]), organized by Chang Ping-lin, Ts'ai Yüan-p'ei, and others, both of which were just as influential as the Hsing Chung Hui. Even after the founding of the Tung Meng Hui, many confusing and competing trends still existed both within and outside the movement.

In his later book, *Li Yüan-hung p'ing-chuan* (A biography of Li Yüan-hung) [206], Shen quotes at some length from various major sources to present a more objective picture of the revolutionary governor of Wuchang, whom Orthodox historians have simply condemned as another opportunistic warlord. By pointing out the subtle political rivalry between the power groups in Wuchang and Nanking during the first months of the Republic, Shen seriously questions the simplistic version of Sun's undisputed leadership in the revolutionary movement.[120]

Shen's other writings cover a wide range of topics from the

part played by certain leading bureaucrats, such as Liang Shih-i, in the engineering of the Manchu abdication[121] to the role of the middle-rank staffs of the revolutionary regimes in 1911-12, such as that of Huang Fu and his associates in Shanghai.[122]

Monographic studies on the constitutionalists by Chang P'eng-yüan [341] and Chang Yü-fa [343], like Shen's works, are encouraging signs of a readiness among Taiwan historians to search for a way to treat the Revolution purely as a historical subject, without polemics and propaganda, although these writers have shown little interest in putting forth new theories or openly questioning many of the basic Orthodox assumptions.

Some articles on Japanese and French attitudes toward the Revolution appearing in the *Ts'ung-k'an* series have further pushed the study of the Revolution to new frontiers. P'eng Tse-chou's articles on Miyazaki Torazo[123] and on the China policy of the Saionji cabinet during 1911[124] demonstrate the research possibilities for the study of the Japanese role in the Revolution. Chang Fu-jui's article on public opinion in France during 1911-12 also breaks new ground.[125]

## INTERNATIONAL COOPERATION

The articles by P'eng and Chang, neither of whom lives in Taiwan, as well as Ssu-yü Teng's writing on secret societies[126] in the same *Ts'ung-k'an* series, provide evidence that the growth of historical study in Taiwan has attracted increasing attention from scholars abroad. Cooperation has been developed between the previously mentioned Academia Sinica's "Oral History" project and its counterpart at Columbia University; historians in Taiwan have been invited to attend international conferences[127]; American scholars and institutions, including the Hoover Institution, are explicitly concerned about the Kuomintang Archives collection on the Revolution; and reports on current developments occasionally appear in foreign periodicals such as the *Newsletter* of the Association for Asian Studies and the *Iho* (Bulletin) of Toyo Bunko's Center for Modern China Studies.

Development in the direction of international communication and cooperation, preliminary as it is, is already bearing fruit. Chang P'eng-yüan's promising study of the late Ch'ing Provincial Assembly is based on the date and the academic discipline he acquired in Taiwan as well as abroad. The studies by Wang Te-chao and Wu Hsiang-hsiang as published in *Ts'ung-k'an* were started as part of the cooperative program sponsored in the fifties by the Far Eastern and Russian Institute of the University of Washington and the History Department of National Taiwan University. And the forthcoming book on Tung Meng Hui by Shelly Cheng is certainly a good example of international, multi-archival research.

In this perspective, then, the publication in 1969 of the eleven-volume Inventory of the Collections at the Party Archives (the main part of [78]) is perhaps the most encouraging sign from Taiwan pointing toward the prospect of modern cataloging and systematic release for scholarly use of the wealth of historical materials on the Revolution under the custody of the Archives. Further steps to open up the collection for scholarly research have been taken in recent years. Under the title of *Chung-hua min-kuo shih-liao ts'ung-pien* (Compendium of sources on the history of the Republic of China), for instance, forty volumes have come out since 1968 containing some twenty-one major sources on the revolutionary movement during the 1900-1912 period. This rapidly growing trend, if one may assume that it will continue, should eventually make scholarship in Taiwan a significant contributing partner in the international community of historical study of modern China in general and of the Revolution in particular.

# — 6 —

# Conclusion:
# A General Evaluation

Having surveyed the main features of the representative works and the trends of historical writings on the Revolution, in this concluding chapter we may turn to a more general assessment of the limitations and contributions of Chinese historiography as a whole. What are the major issues that the Chinese writings have illuminated and in which areas have they contributed substantially to our knowledge? What are the approaches and research possibilities that deserve serious consideration but have been hitherto little explored by Chinese historians?

One of the chief contributions of many Chinese writers, I think, is that they highlight the role of the Hsing Chung Hui in the revolutionary movement. For example, however much historians may qualify the vague political ideas expressed by Hsing Chung Hui members, the phrase "to establish a republican government" in the oath which every Hsing Chung Hui member has been required to pledge since 1895 marks the beginning of a new type of opposition movement in China. Although Hsing Chung Hui bears the distinct imprint of the secret-society tradition in China, the concept of founding a republic is in clear contrast with the traditional goals of the secret-society rebellions. In these rebellions the leaders usually exploited the deep-rooted faith of the peasant masses in monarchical rule. A rebel leader would claim himself to be either the rightful heir of the preceding Ming dynasty, or the emperor of a coming dynasty with the heavenly mandate on his side, or the legitimate ruler of the present throne who had escaped and hidden from the usurper's hands and was now reappearing to lead a restoration campaign. A very similar tradition may be found in the Pugachev rebellion as well as in many other peasant uprisings in tsarist Russia.

It is from this viewpoint of ideological breakthrough that the Hsing Chung Hui may indeed be distinguished from other contemporary secret societies, even if one may question whether Hsing Chung Hui did in fact play such a leading role in the years preceding the founding of the Tung Meng Hui in 1905 as depicted by many Orthodox historians. It is also from the ideological angle that both the Orthodox and the Neo-Orthodox schools have most convincingly demonstrated that the Revolution was more than another rebellion of the traditional type.

Chinese writings, however, do not further advance the study of the ideological problems involved in the Revolution. They have thrown little light on the intellectual issues of early twentieth-century China. Although there is no lack of Chinese writings on the polemical battles engaged in by Liang Ch'i-ch'ao and the Tung Meng Hui revolutionaries in Tokyo, few scholars have seriously probed the intellectual reservoir of the debates. Much valuable material could surely be discovered in the Japanese intellectual history of the Meiji era, especially in those works that exerted a direct influence on Liang Ch'i-ch'ao and on the Tung Meng Hui thinkers. Nor has there been much effort to explore beyond the general and vague assertions on the subject of the relationship between the Tokyo émigrés and the central stream of intellectual discussions in China proper. In particular, little investigation has been made of the concerns and the thinking of the constitutionalist gentry who before 1911 had not advocated a revolution but whose influence in the shaping of the general course of the Revolution during the 1911-12 period was overwhelming. By placing great emphasis on the leadership of the Tung Meng Hui and by simply denouncing the constitutionalist gentry and the Ch'ing bureaucrats as opportunists, neither school offers any satisfactory explanation for the shift in political allegiance of these elite groups during the 1911 Revolution.

In various reminiscent accounts by revolutionary participants, however, there exists ample evidence of a certain strong sentiment, or concern, which provided a common ground for their cooperation with the constitutionalists. On the surface, their concern was manifested, first, in worry about foreign encroachment, or, still worse, about the eventual foreign partition of China; and second, in contempt for the incompetency of the Manchu regime. More fundamentally, this concern reflected the rise of a new and distinct sense of responsibility among educated Chinese. Many of them seem to have been committed to the idea that it was they themselves rather than the emperor or the courtiers in Peking who were ultimately responsible for the survival and prosperity of China. And it was their desire for change and progress, as well as their sense of urgency, that most clearly distinguished this group from the traditional official-gentry-scholars. Representatives of this new educated group may be found among treaty-port journalists, provincial assemblymen, students studying abroad, members of the civil bureaucracy, and even among the New Army officers. As a class, it cuts across the Neo-Orthodox class divisions.

The opinions and actions within this group suggest, of course, a wide spectrum of viewpoints, with the revolutionaries generally standing at the extreme left, and the constitutionalist gentry ranging from the middle to the right. The general concern about the fate of China, however, not only turned many constitutionalists to the revolutionary camp during 1911-12 but also explains why the revolutionary cause espoused by the Wuchang soldiers evoked among the educated classes an immediate and nationwide sympathetic response.

Although such a commonly shared intellectual concern was clearly manifest in contemporary writings of the 1900s, the bias and prejudice of leading revolutionaries prevented the Orthodox school, at its formative stage, from taking a view that would put on an equal footing with the revolutionaries those constitutionalist leaders who had sided with Yüan in his 1913 struggle against the revolutionaries. Later, the dominance of this school in turn prevented historians from taking a more objective view. It is no less difficult for the Neo-Orthodox school to handle the ideological commitment of this educated class, which sometimes cannot be comfortably fitted into the Marxian conceptual scheme.

Side by side with ideological changes, institutional transformation is another promising field for future study of the Revolution. From the viewpoint of social change, an ideological movement, like a storm sweeping over the land, may have no lasting effect unless many of the ideas and values it has advocated are institutionalized. Moreover, the disintegration of the old systems often begins long before the actual eruption of a revolution and, in turn, facilitates shifts in the realm of ideas and values. However, it is to this institutional aspect that Chinese historians of the Revolution have paid the least attention. The traditional emphasis on personal virtues and personal ties is found in many writings. The best of these reveal the authors' ambitious attempts to outline the maze of personal relationships during the Revolution. Such an emphasis, important as it is, often blinds historians to the social and economic factors at work. The representatives of the Neo-Orthodox school, equipped with Marxist-Leninist theories, could have blazed new trails for the study of institutional changes had their energy and time not been absorbed in futile quibbling over doctrinal interpretation.

One consequence of this absence of scholarly works on the aspect of social change is that the general isolation of the Manchu state from Chinese society in the last decades of the Ch'ing dynasty has been totally neglected. By its reluctance to accept a constitutional monarchy, and by remaining satisfied with conducting an essentially reactionary domestic policy focused on the maintenance of traditional power, the throne forfeited many of its functions to the moderate and radical elements of society. To be sure, there was no lack of vigor in the court-sponsored reforms during the 1906-11 period, but it may well be asked whether these reforms were tried too late to save the Manchu court. Much of the local government in the cities and in the countryside, as well as a great part of the economic activity and most of the intellectual and cultural development of China, seems to have fallen into the hands of social groups who were acting independently of the Manchu regime and often in opposition to it. These elements established control over a very considerable area of the country's domestic life, and thereby weakened the regime's hold long before 1911.

From another angle, one may ask also whether such court-sponsored reforms paradoxically contributed to the revolutionary forces. The enormous tax increase, for instance, as an immediate result of the late Ch'ing reforms, aroused much resentment among the populace, and sparked the various resistance movements not only of the peasants but also of the gentry and the merchant class. "The reforms" as Mary C. Wright observes, "thus added to the growing revolutionary pressures in society in two ways: by the new forces they set in motion and by the resistance they generated—resistance not to their goals but to the only means the imperial government had to achieve them."[128]

The questions we have been raising cannot be adequately answered without serious studies of the local government, of the New Army, of modern schooling, and of the financial and economic institutions introduced during the years preceding the Revolution. Such studies could shed much light upon the rapid and easy secession of provincial centers from the Manchu empire.

That the Revolution may be regarded as a "social revolution" is implied in our raising these various problems to illustrate the research possibilities concerning the Revolution's ideological and institutional aspects. This view of a social revolution has generally been accepted, either explicitly or

implicitly, in many Chinese writings, even though no definitive study has yet been undertaken. Both the Orthodox and the
Neo-Orthodox schools are unsatisfied with the view that the
1911-12 events were simply a racial conflict or an anti-dynastic
rebellion. The Neo-Orthodox school in particular has devoted
much attention to the problems of the bourgeoisie and of other
classes throughout the course of the Revolution. However, a
scholar, setting out to prove or disprove that 1911 marked the
beginning of a social revolution, and trying to gain an understanding of the scope and the depth of the Revolution's social
significance, would not necessarily find the class approach
more rewarding than the ideological or the institutional
approach. On the one hand, a determination of whether or not
certain classes either did or did not participate in the Revolution is neither necessary nor would it be sufficient, for that
matter, to settle the issue of whether the Revolution was in
fact a social revolution. It is not necessary because even if the
bourgeoisie or certain other classes did not play a major part,
the 1911-12 events may still be interpreted as a social revolution; and it is not sufficient because, given widespread discontent within a certain class (e.g., the peasantry) on the eve of
the Revolution, such discontent need not have burst forth in
the form of a modern revolution. It could have fallen into the
traditional pattern of peasant rebellion, such as the White
Lotus, the Niens, the Boxers, or innumerable other uprisings
in Chinese history. On the other hand, the extent and depth
of the social influence of the Revolution may be much more
effectively determined by the findings of an investigation into
the changes that occurred in the realms of social values and
social institutions.

The Chinese historiography of the past half-century has
also depicted the Revolution as generally ''modern,'' or
''Western,'' in outlook. By stressing the importance of Sun
Yat-sen's role in the whole movement, the Orthodox school
projected a Western image of the Revolution. The dominance
of this view has since 1927 prevented Chinese writers from
interpreting the Revolution in the perspective of dynastic

cycles, a perspective so familiar to Chinese historians as to have become stereotyped. In the meantime, however, this modernistic view has blinded people to many traditional features of the revolutionary movement, e.g. the role of the secret societies. The Neo-Orthodox school has inherited this view and has fortified it with the theories that grew out of the specific experiences of Western Europe.

To compare the 1911 Revolution with the French Revolution or with other cases in European history is certainly illuminating; but in comparing two revolutions or any other two events, we would do well to examine both similarities and differences. By emphasizing only the similarities, however, Chinese historians have generally shelved those unique features of the Revolution that are in sharp contrast with European examples.

When the focus of attention is shifted to the traditional features, then the revolutionary movement appears no longer a monolithic one, simple and clear-cut. From the complicated and confusing phenomena there emerge signs pointing for example to an interesting shift, in terms of revolutionary strategies, goals, and styles, from a more traditional to a more European pattern. For instance, the nature of the earlier uprisings, which Sun sponsored directly, is in sharp contrast with many of the 1911 uprisings. The early uprisings relied heavily upon secret-society organization, with most of the participants coming from the lower classes. In order to avoid a direct confrontation with government forces, they limited their sphere of activity mainly to the countryside, especially to the border areas of administrative units. A typical example was the Waichow Uprising of 1900. On the other hand, the Canton Uprising in the spring of 1911 and the Wuchang Uprising in the following autumn were conducted mainly by the younger generation of the educated class, including New Army officers and students returning from abroad. Their focus of attention was on the administrative and urban centers; and they were often anxious to stage a dramatic, direct confrontation with Manchu authority.

If the earlier uprisings suggest the pattern of the traditional rebellion, as the one manifested in those of the White Lotus and the Nien, the student-revolutionaries consciously modeled their efforts on European examples. While the peasant uprisings were always given impetus by the desire for a better life and, in several cases, induced by the promise of immediate material rewards, the intellectual revolutionaries were often concerned about national issues and inspired by lofty idealism. Sometimes, too, they were fascinated by foreign examples of martyrdom and assassination.

It is beyond the scope of this study to discuss the two patterns in detail. In many instances actual events were far more complicated than may be indicated within the confines of this summary. With all these qualifications in mind we may still, however, distinguish the two types. And by keeping our eyes on the mainstream of the revolutionary movement, we may readily trace the shift of Tung Meng Hui's strategy from the first type to the second.

Throughout our discussion about the shifts and the stream in the revolutionary movement, the importance of the time dimension is implied. To neglect this dimension, as occurs all too frequently in Chinese writings, may result in as serious a distortion of the Revolution as a phoenix woven into a tapestry: elaborate in detail but flat and lifeless. With the time dimension added, however, there seems to emerge a new perspective; and the long and complex revolutionary movement then appears, at each of its many stages, to have had different scopes, varying degrees of momentum, and shifting emphases on revolutionary goals.

At the earliest stage, small groups of intellectuals, imbued with some Western ideas, attempted to exploit the traditional secret-society uprisings without necessarily revealing their goals to the members of these societies. After the founding of the Tung Meng Hui in 1905, however, the revolutionary movement became part of a broad intellectual movement, of which the ultimate concerns were the survival and transformation of China. Since the Manchu throne was regarded as blocking the way to a strengthening of China, the anti-Manchu issue was very often associated with the anti-imperialist issue. Thus, at some point or another in the writings of the 1900-11 period Neo-Orthodox historians have been able to find readily whatever they wanted to prove. When the center of the movement drifted to the left, the Tung Meng Hui had the opportunity to seize leadership, but the movement remained essentially an intellectual one, with little significant power struggle involved. Among the student-revolutionaries of China, as in revolutionary movements of other countries, there was no want of examples of scandals or of opportunism or of evidence of excessive vanity and other moral frailty. But it is undeniable that these arrogant and quarrelsome young men and women had genuine intellectual concerns and were not lacking in lofty idealism.

However, the revolutionary incident of 1911-12, which led to the downfall of the Manchu dynasty, was not merely another episode in the intellectual movement, but involved very real and very tough power struggles. Although patriotic concerns and idealistic elements still loomed large, the decisive factors, as the course of events rapidly proved, were now personal ambition and security, the concerns of the military establishment, the commitment to local order, and the desire to perpetuate autonomous provincial power. Consequently, the period witnessed a series of power struggles and political maneuvers: provincial secessions from the Manchu empire, rivalry within the revolutionary camp, army mutinies, assassinations, secret negotiations between the revolutionaries and Yüan Shih-k'ai, the forced abdication of the Emperor, and Yüan's ascendancy to the presidency. All these fascinating stories, told and retold by Chinese historians, bear much resemblance to events that presaged the end of many earlier dynasties.

Nevertheless, to distinguish the 1911-12 incident from the earlier revolutionary movement does not necessarily lead to the conclusion that the incident was not part of a modern revolution. By liquidating the monarchical system, the incident of 1911-12 not only legitimized many of the institutional and ideological changes that had long been under way, but also created new possibilities for further changes. Writers like Shang Ping-ho, who regarded the Revolution as merely a dynastic rebellion, were focusing their view on the 1911-12 power struggle rather than surveying the longer process of social revolution. On the other hand, those who were proud of the idealistic aspect of the intellectual movement tended to reduce the incident to one revolutionary episode. In short, from different perspectives we may get different impressions of the 1911 Revolution. In its broadest sense, the Revolution may be said to have started as a movement sponsored by small groups of intellectuals, but to have finally developed into a large-scale political and social process of which the 1911-12 incident, or the Revolution in its narrowest sense, stands as a landmark in a long journey. While historians have the right to choose the viewpoint they consider adequate, it would seem that the omission of the time dimension from the complex process of the Revolution does violence to historical discipline.

# Notes

(In the following notes, bracketed numbers refer to entry numbers in the Bibliography.)

1. It is generally accepted that this tradition has dominated Chinese historiography ever since the T'ang dynasty (A.D. 618-906). See Naito Torajiro, *Shina shigaku shi* (A history of Chinese historiography), Tokyo, 1949, pp. 236-40; and Chin Yü-fu, *Chung-kuo shih-hsüeh shih* (A history of Chinese historiography), Peking, 1962, pp. 73-74, 97-98. For a comprehensive English survey of Chinese historiography in traditional times, see W.G. Beasley and E.G. Pulleyblank, eds., *Historians of China and Japan,* London, 1961.

2. See Lien-sheng Yang, "The Organization of Chinese Official Historiography: Principles and Methods of Standard Histories from the T'ang through the Ming Dynasty," in Beasley and Pulleyblank, eds., pp. 44-59.

3. For the traditional influence on modern Chinese historiography see, for instance, the review articles which John K. Fairbank and Mary C. Wright edited under the title "Documentary Collection on Modern Chinese History: An Introduction," *JAS* 17 (Nov. 1957): 55-111. For a comprehensive bibliographic survey of the works produced from the Chinese mainland in the fifties and early sixties, see Albert Feuerwerker and Sally Cheng, *Chinese Communist Studies of*

*Modern Chinese History* (Cambridge, Mass., 1961). For discussions on specific topics, see the essays written for the International Conference on Chinese Communist Historiography held in Oxfordshire, England, in Sept. 1964, which were first published in the 1965 and 1966 issues of *China Quarterly* and subsequently anthologized in Albert Feuerwerker, ed., *History in Communist China* (Cambridge, Mass., 1968).

4. For the major sources of these canons, see [5], [209], and [237].

5. The innumerable articles, speeches, and pamphlets on the Three People's Principles produced during the Republican period are not included in this survey because they generally belonged to the realm of party polemicists. The Orthodox historians usually avoided polemics and accepted Sun's own opinions as expressed in *Chung-kuo ko-ming shih* [209] and in his lecture, *The Three People's Principles*, which are to be found in all the major collections of his works such as [211], [212] and [215].

6. For the major themes of the Neo-Orthodox school, see [147], vol. 4. This volume was compiled and edited by Liu Ta-nien and other members of Chung-kuo k'o-hsüeh-yuan (Chinese Academy of Science). See also [2], vol. 1, Preface, [28], and [268].

7. Marie-Claire Bergère, "La Révolution de 1911 jugée par les historiens de la République populaire de Chine: Thèmes et controverses," *Revue Historique* (Paris), Oct.-Dec. 1963, p.408.

8. For example, there are accounts about revolutionary martyrdom in [307] and biographical works on Hsü Hsi-lin and other revolutionaries in *Min Pao* [322].

9. Such as Huang Min's *Ch'iu feng ch'iu yü* (A windy and rainy autumn), 2 vols. (Shanghai, 1907); and *Ch'iu Chin* ([A biography of] Ch'iu Chin), 1907, author and place of publication unknown. For further bibliographic information on these books see [2], 8: 673-74.

10. A representative work is Chang Hsing-yen, *Su-pao an chi-shih* (An account of the Su Pao case [13], which was later

reprinted under the title of *Kuei-mao ta-yü chi* (The great lawsuit of 1903). For a similar booklet on the "March 29th" uprising, see [112].

11. Miyazaki Torazo's autobiography was first published in Tokyo in 1902 under the title *Sanjūsannen no yume* (The thirty-three years' dream). Incidentally, Sun Yat-sen's Chinese preface to the first Japanese edition of this work, written in 1902, is among the earliest of his available writings on the Revolution.

12. The Chinese version [194], which includes only the sections on the revolutionary movement centering around Sun Yat-sen's career, contains less than one-fourth of the writings in the original Japanese version. The Peking reprint in [2] has corrected certain typographical errors. The Taipei reprint is a photoreproduction of the 1906 edition containing Liu Kuang-han's brief essay, which is not included in [2].

13. Before Lo's study appeared, several close associates of Sun had already begun to question the reliability of the account given in *Kidnapped in London*. In 1929 Ch'en Shao-pai mentioned a different version of the kidnapping incident given by Sun (see [34]). About the same time, Wu Chih-hui published in *Hsien-tai p'ing-lün* ([301], vol. 2, no. 30 [July 1925]: 9-11) still another version of the incident rendered by Wu Tsung-lien, an official of the Ch'ing Legation to London. Wu's account is included in [178].

14. In the months following the Wuchang Uprising in 1911, *Min-li pao* [321] published, in addition to news dispatches, lengthy accounts of uprisings in regional centers such as Wuchang (Oct. 14-Nov.18 and Nov.26-27), Shanghai (Nov.4-17), Nanking (Nov.13), Canton (Nov.13-17), Foochow (Nov.20), Changsha (Nov.17,19,22, and 28), Kiukiang (Nov.5), and in Manchuria (Dec.22-24). It published also biographical sketches of revolutionary leaders like Sun Yat-sen (Nov.23), Ts'ai Yüan-p'ei (Jan.9-10, 1912) and Li Yüan-hung (Oct.16, 1911), as well as accounts of revolutionary martyrs (Dec.4 and 21-22, 1911; Jan.29 and Oct.10 and 13, 1912).

15. Such as *Tung-fang tsa-chih* ([336], vol. 8, no. 8 [Oct.

1911]-vol. 8, no. 12 [June 1912]), and various issues of *Shih-shih hsin-pao*. Many articles on the Revolution from *Shih-shih hsin-pao* were later anthologized in [201].

16. Among the major works of a documentary nature produced in the 1911-12 period, the following is not accessible, as far as we can ascertain, to scholars outside the Chinese mainland: Po-hai shou-min, pseud., comp. *Hsin-hai ko-ming shih-mo chi* (A full account of the 1911 Revolution), 12 vols. (Shanghai, 1912). This is a compilation of contemporary documents and news reports on the Revolution during the first six months following the Wuchang Uprising.

17. Such as [44], [101], [186], [228] and [282].

18. Cheng Lieh's work on the martyrdom of the "March 29" incident [36] is a representative one. A less accessible work of this kind is *Chiao Ch'en shih-lu* (A true account of the case of Chiao [Ta-feng] and Ch'en [Tso-hsin]), published in Shanghai in 1912 by *Min-chüan pao* (Democracy daily), an organ of the revolutionists.

19. The members of Wen Hsüeh She (Literary Society), for example, compiled the *Ko-ming t'uan-t'i Wen-hsüeh-she ti li-shih* (The history of Wen Hsüeh She, a revolutionary organization). The work was first published as a serial in [321], May-June 1912, and then reproduced in a single volume under the general editorship of Li Shih-yüeh. The major portion of the work may be found in [162], which is a later work by Li.

20. Such works as [14] and [171] treat the Revolution cynically, but the major works written from an anti-revolutionary viewpoint, like [267], did not appear until 1916, when it was all too clear that the Republican government had been wracked by Yüan's monarchical strivings.

21. See [82], I, Preface, pp. 9-13 [separately paginated], and [86], I, Preface, pp.5-6.

22. For Sun's life in exile in Japan, see Marius Jansen, *The Japanese and Sun Yat-sen* (Cambridge, Mass., 1954).

23. For a general picture, see [153]. For Sun's bitterest experiences in warlord politics, see Winston Hsieh, "The

Ideas and Ideals of a Warlord—Ch'en Chung-ming," in *Papers on China*, 16 (Cambridge, Mass., 1962): 198-252.

24. Huang Hsing and many other leading revolutionaries refused to take an oath pledging loyalty to Sun and did not join Sun's new party in 1914. For details, see Chün-tu Hsüeh, *Huang Hsing and the Chinese Revolution*, (Stanford, Calif. 1961), pp.164-68. Huang and some other exiled revolutionary leaders even stopped the anti-Yüan campaign temporarily while Yüan was facing the crisis of Japan's Twenty-one Demands. On 25 Feb. 1915 they issued a long circular telegram in which they pledged not to use foreign powers to overthrow Yüan's government. The telegram was copied in Hu Shih, *Hu Shih liu-hsüeh jih-chi* (The diary of Hu Shih's student life in the United States), 4 vols. (Shanghai, 1947), 3:661-18.

25. One example is the entente between some southwestern warlords and the moderate wing, especially the Cheng-hsüeh-hsi (Political Study Clique), of the Kuomintang, an entente which eventually forced Sun to leave Canton in 1918. For details, see [152] or its abridged English translation, *The Political History of China, 1840-1928* (trans. by S.Y.Teng and J. Ingalls, Princeton, 1956), pp. 312-88.

26. One major group which competed with Sun in the overseas Chinese communities was Ou-shih yen-chiu hui (Society for the Study of European Affairs) which developed later into the Cheng-hsüeh-hsi (which is mentioned in footnote 25). Another group consisting mainly of Kwangtung revolutionaries was Shui-li yen-chiu she (Society for Irrigation Studies). Information on their rivalry with Sun's party may be found in (a) the account in [184] given by Sun's group, pp. 10-12; (b) Chü Cheng's circular letter to the members of the Chung-hua ko-ming-tang (Chinese Revolutionary Party) in [55], 1:238-40; and (c) Yeh Hsia-sheng's reminiscent account in [280], pp. 80-82.

27. [201], Preface, p.1.

28. Ibid.

29. Among other journals and newspapers, they founded *Min-kuo tsa-chih* (Republican Magazine) in Tokyo in 1914,

*Chien-she* (Construction) in Shanghai in 1919, and *Hsin chien-she* (New construction) in Shanghai in 1923. Among the publishing houses they founded in these years was Min-chih shu-chü (People's Enlightenment Book Co.) in Shanghai, which produced various historical works on the Revolution.

30. Tsou Lu and some other Kwangtung revolutionaries started to collect materials on the ''March 29'' Uprising around 1918. By 1920 their project had developed into the Committee for the Investigation of the Huang-hua-kang Martyrdom in Canton (Kuang-chou Huang-hua-kang lieh-shih shen-ch'a hui) and by 1926 into the Society for the Commemoration of the Revolution (Ko-ming chi-nien-hui). For information on the project, see Tsou's letters and reports in [138], pp.112-23.

31. The book was withdrawn from public circulation soon after being reprinted in Taipei in 1962 because it was charged that it was anti-revolutionary and too sympathetic to the Manchus and to Yüan Shih-k'ai. (Details are given in Chapter V.) The historians on the mainland having preserved many of the Orthodox views, also regard the book as ''defending Yüan Shih-k'ai'' and as ''partial to the constitutionalists'' (see [2], 8: 643).

32. See the prefaces to the book; [202], pp. 1-5. The esteem in which traditional historians held the book may be judged from these facts: Several of its biographical accounts of revolutionaries were later included in [193], the leading biographical encyclopedia of the early republican period; some were published in a textbook of classical Chinese; and many other parts were used as models by later biographers; for this information, see Liang Jung-jo, ''Ch'ien-yen'' (Introduction) in the Taipei reprint of [202].

33. For the full citation of this work, see [153]; and for the revised and enlarged version, see [152]. A comparison of the two versions shows that there is no change at all in the chapters on the revolutionary movement, on Sun Yat-sen's career, and on the warlord politics, though the last chapter of the earlier version, which contains some socialistic and liberal

views, is omitted and brief summaries of nineteenth-century history are added in the revised version. The abridged English version prepared by S.Y. Teng and J. Ingalls is based on [152].

34. Several of Chang's writings on the Su Pao case, on the Kuang Fu Hui, and on the Hankow Uprising launched by Tzu-li chün in 1900 were later published in the Communist-sponsored compendium, *Hsin-hai ko-ming* (see [2], 1:253-57, 280-81, 367-86, 391-97, and 521-29). For bibliographic information on Chang's unpublished manuscripts, see [2], 8:624-25.

35. For example, [189] is a collection of biographical sketches of Sun by leading Nationalist figures in the 1920s. For a longer work, see [76].

36. For example [215] is still cited in recent publications.

37. For Tsou's revolutionary career, see [238], especially vol. 1, although his role in the revolutionary movement is understandably exaggerated in the book.

38. In the forties Tsou revised and enlarged the work mainly by adding to it many biographical accounts of revolutionaries (see [237]).

39. Feng's "Hsing-chung-hui tsu-chih shih" (A historical account of the organization of the Hsing Chung Hui) remains the most comprehensive account of the subject. It is included in [86] , vol. 4, and in [2], vol. 3.

40. See [86], I, Preface, p.5.

41. For full citation, [68]. For another example, see [77].

42. A representative work is Liu Lu-yin, "Ko-ming yü fan-ko-ming" (Revolution and counterrevolution), in *Ko'ming yü fan-ko-ming* (Revolution and counterrevolution), edited by Lang Hsing-shih (Shanghai, 1928), pp.447-52.

43. See [82], I:iv.

44. For an elaborate edition of such works, see [92].

45. For Sun's comment, see [190], *chüan* 3, pp. 17-18; and Shen Yun-lung, "Ch'en Ying-shih yü Huang K'o-ch'iang" (Ch'en Ch'i-mei and Huang Hsing), in [204], pp.77-119.

46. Sonoda Kazukama, *Shina shinjin kokuki* (New figures

in China) (Tokyo, 1927); Chinese translation by Huang Hui-ch'uan and others (Shanghai, 1930), p. 267.

47. Sun Yat-sen, *Tsung-li ch'üan chi* (Collected works of Sun Yat-sen) (Taipei, 1951), 8:11.

48. [2], 3:52. For Ch'en's conflict with Chang Ch'ien and other gentry leaders over the murder of a revolutionist leader by a Manchu official who was protected by the gentry leaders from legal prosecution, see Liu Ya-tzu, "Yüan lieh-shih Meng-t'ao chüan" (Biography of martyr Yüan Meng-t'ao), quoted in [204], p. 100; and the legal documents in [264], *chüan* 1, pp.20b-28, and *chüan* 2, pp. 1-8.

49. Such as Shao Yüan-ch'ung, "Hsing chuang" (Biography [of Ch'en Ch'i-mei]), in [92], *chüan* 4, pp.1-5b. For other eulogies, see *ibid.*, *chüan* 4, pp. 7-19.

50. Several persons signed the petition to the Kuomintang party authority for suppressing Ts'ao's book. According to Feng Tzu-yu, the pressure came mainly from two Wu brothers from Hupeh, Wu Hsing-han and Wu Hsing-ya, who charged that Ts'ao had exaggerated the contributions of Jih Chih Hui and had deliberately played down the role of Wu's group in revolutionary history (see [86] 2:58-61). Wu Hsing-han did later attack the book in an article, "Wu-ch'ang ch'i-i san-jih chi" (A three-day account of the Wuchang Uprising), in [73], 5:78-98. Some surviving revolutionaries from Hupeh did, however, tell me that the suppression stemmed partly also from pressures exerted by Hu I-sheng, a Cantonese revolutionist who was a cousin of Hu Han-min. In a long circular report issued right after the abortive "March 29th" Uprising, Hu I-sheng had been unjustly charged by Huang Hsing with failure to carry out his duty during the Uprising. Ts'ao unwisely published the full text of Huang's report in his book ([232], 1:327-47). For the background of Huang's report, see [73], 3:39-40 (separately paginated). A number of advance copies of Ts'ao's book survived the political persecution, and the Hoover Library has one copy. Some parts of the book (on the Jih Chih Hui and the Wuchang Uprising) are reprinted in [2] 1:572-86, and 5:104-68. Meanwhile, some senior party members from Fukien were instrumental in suppressing another book on the Revolution [145], as

mentioned in the Preface and Chapter One of [346].

51. See discussions on Chang Nan-hsien's writings, in particular pp. 35-36.

52. Such as Chang Yin-lin's comment (see [315], vol. 1, no.4, p.96).

53. [315], vol. 1, no. 4, pp.93-96.

54.[315], vol. 1, no. 2, pp.79-85.

55. For the text of the petition and for Chin Yü-fu's article on *Ch'ing-shih-kao,* see [315], vol. 1, no. 3, pp. 25-54.

56. See Li Hsi-pin, "Ch'ing-mo Chih-na an-sha-t'uan chi-shih (A factual account of the China Assassination Corps in the late Ch'ing period), in [141], pp.17-23.

57. [315], vol.1, no.1, pp.44-56.

58. [17], pp.414-16.

59. Both as an important member of Tung Meng Hui and as a revolutionary from Hupeh, Chü played a very active role in 1911-12. His memoirs, under the titles of "Hsin-hai cha-chi" and "Mei-ch'uan jih-chi," are valuable sources on both the revolutionary movement in Hupeh and on the Provisional Government in Nanking. For a recent reprint of his memoirs, see [55], 2:469-576.

60. For the full citation of Li's work, see [159]. Li had access to many reliable materials on the revolutionary movement in Hupeh, because he served as the chief secretary of the revolutionary government in Wuchang in the first week following the Uprising and later headed the office for the compilation of the gazetteer of Hupeh province.

61. For the full citation of Hu's work, see [116]. Hu reports his experiences in both Hupeh and Hopeh during the eventful 1911-12 periods. His speculation about Wang Ching-wei's obscure contact with Yüan Shih-k'ai is interesting, but he probably under-reports the contact between Yüan and Wuchang Governor Li Yüan-hung, who sent Hu as a secret envoy to the north in 1911.

62. For Hu's major works, see [120] and [121].

63. One work of great reference value is Chiang Ch'ün's oral account rendered in 1940 to the KMT Committee on

Party History about the secession of Kiangsi province in 1911
from Manchu rule (see [73], vol. 4:74-88). The manuscripts of two
other reminiscent accounts on the revolutionary movement in
Kiangsi, [254] and [272], are in the East Asian Collection of the
Hoover Institution.

64. Several important writings on the Su Pao incident and on
the part played by intellectuals are included in [71] and [185].

65. The main feature of the revised and enlarged version
is the fourth volume, in which some five hundred pages are
devoted exlusively to "biographical writings," or *lieh-chuan*,
on 227 individuals who played an active part in the revolutionary movement. In addition, Tsou supplies hitherto unpublished details in his accounts of various uprisings. For specific
bibliographic information on editions and dates, see [237].

66. According to the publisher's preface to the Taipei
reprint of Feng's *History* ([82], vol. 1, 1954), Feng finished
writing the later part of the book in two more volumes, the
first of which was published in Chungking in 1946. But the
other volume has never been published, and the manuscript is
probably in Taipei.

67. Some parts of the book [86] are included in both [2]
and [73]. Many of the sections were first published as articles
in journals such as [309] and [331]. For additional bibliographical information, see the author's preface to each volume.
See also Chang's bibliographical remarks in [2], 8:612-13,
though his notes on editions and dates are in several places
inaccurate.

68. For example, the third volume contains a carefully
compiled list of over two hundred titles of revolutionary publications in the 1899-1911 period, with the name of editor/
publisher, date, and place noted. The author's nostalgia led
him to include in the list many famous but non-revolutionary
publications and even the works of K'ang Yu-wei's group (see
3:139-60).

69. For the formation of the Committee and its initial
work, see "Ti pa pien: Shih-liao pien-ch'uan" (Part 8: Compilation of historical materials), in *Min-kuo erh-shih-san nien*

*chung-kuo kuo-min-tang nien-chien* (Chinese Nationalist Party's Year Book: 1934) (Nanking, 1934).

70. The publications under the Committee's sponsorship include [311] and [334].

71. See Chapter 5, pp. 65-68.

72. Some memoirs by participants appeared in [312].

73. Ch'en Tu-hsiu, "Tzu-chan chieh-chi ti ko-ming yü ko-ming ti tzu-ch'an chieh-chi" (The bourgeois revolution and the revolutionary bourgeoisie), first published in [300], no. 22, 23 April 1923; later included in [105], pp. 51-61.

74. [105], p.54.

75. See Peng Shuh-chih, "Shui shih Chung-kuo kuo-min ko-ming chih lin-tao che" (Who is the leader of the Chinese national revolution?), first published in [303], 20 Dec. 1924; later included in [105], pp.3-31.

76. See Chih-shen, pseud. (Chu Chih-hsin), "Te-i-chih she-hui ko-ming-chia hsiao-chuan" (Biographical sketches of German socialist revolutionaries), [322], no. 2 (May 1905), pp. 1-18 [s.p.].

77. See Ch'ü's discussions in [56]. For a succinct English summary of the controversies, see Benjamin I. Schwartz, *Chinese Communism and the Rise of Mao* (Cambridge, Mass., 3rd printing, 1958), pp. 68-70.

78. The work is included in [148].

79. [122], Preface, p.1.

80. To give two examples, *Ch'ün-chung* (The Masses) devoted two special issues to a discussion of the Chinese people's *min-tzu-hsing* ("national character"), vol. 8, nos. 11-12 (July-Aug. 1943); and a new journal, *Chung-kuo wen-hua* (Chinese culture), was inaugurated in Yenan in 1940.

81. See Mao, *Hsin min-chu chu-i lun* (On new democracy) (Yenan, 1940). The item is included in almost every anthology of Mao's works. *Chung-kuo ko ming yü Chung-kuo kung ch'an tang* (The Chinese Revolution and the Chinese Communist Party), which is also included in many anthologies of Mao's works, advances the same theme but gives less attention to the 1911 Revolution.

82. The Hoover East Asian Collection has copies of [61], [175], and a few other samples.

83. For example, see *Chieh-fang jih-pao*, 8-12 Oct. 1942. Original copies exist in Hoover East Asian Collection.

84. For a discussion of the restrictions on free archival research and of the tradition of official control of historical records, see also L.S. Yang's article in Beasley and Pulleyblank, eds., *Historians of China and Japan*, pp. 44-59.

85. For the English review articles on the first eight series of these collections, see *Journal of Asian Studies* (Nov. 1957), pp.55-112.

86. Such as [66], [269], and [271]. Records of field investigations and oral-history interviews conducted by the History department of Yangchow Teacher's College, for instance, are included in [269].

87. Such as [207] and [274].

88. Many such writings are included in [191] and [192].

89. For a leading bibliographical guide to historical writings on the Revolution, see [67].

90. See [8], [9], and [10] for bibliographical information on the series. Some less accessible bibliographies, e.g., [43], [86], and [136], are reprinted in [8]; and in [9] there is the up-to-date bibliography by Chang Tz'u-hsi, which affords more detail than the *HHKM* bibliographies.

91. [41], [42], [43], and articles such as "Ch'ing-mo hsiao-shuo tza-chih lüeh" (A brief survey of novels and journals in the late Ch'ing), [8], I:103-10.

92. The bibliography was first published in *Hsüeh Lin* (April 1941) vol. 6; then partially reprinted in [8], I:97-103; its revised version was included in [43].

93. Such as [28], [147], vol. 4, and [268].

94. Such periodicals include [292], [317], and the historical journals published by various universities.

95. See [318], 1961, nos. 4 and 6; 1962, nos. 1-2, 4-6.

96. For a résumé of the discussions at the Conference, see "Hsin-hai ko-ming wu-shih-chou-nien hsueh-shu t'ao-lun hui t'ao-lun ti i-hsieh wen-t'i" (Issues discussed at the Research Conference in celebration of the jubilee of the 1911 Revolution), [318],

1961, no. 6, pp.6-19. Many of the Conference papers, together with the résumé, were first published in [318] and later included in [117].

97. The rivalry between the two orientations was of course manifested before 1963. For example, Chien Po-chan's attacks on Shang Yueh are the best evidence of this rivalry (see Chien's article in [318], 1960, no. 3, pp. 1-3). For the discussions on "historicism vs. class-viewpoints" see Ning-k'o's article in [318], 1963, no.4, and Kuan Feng and Lin Yü-shih's article in [318], 1963, no. 6.

98. Harold Kahn and Albert Feuerwerker, "The Ideology of Scholarship—China's New Historiography," *China Quarterly* (April-June 1965), pp.1-13. Reprinted in Feuerwerker, ed., *History in Communist China,* pp.1-13.

99. [318], 1963, no. 3, pp. 1-26.

100. [117], pp. 10-55.

101. [117], pp. 56-98.

102. For the viewpoints expressed at the discussion sessions, see the résumé published in [318], 1961, no. 6, or in [117].

103. [318], 1962, no. 1, pp. 126-27.

104. [117], pp. 115-46.

105. See [318], 1961, no. 5, or [117], pp. 188-203.

106. [117], pp. 323-53.

107. See Hou Wai-lu and Chao Chi-pin, *Chin-tai Chung-kuo ssu-hsiang hsueh-shuo shih* (An intellectual history of modern China), Ch. 16; and Wan Wei-ch'eng, " Chang T'ai-yen ti ssu-hsiang" (The thought of Chang Ping-lin), in *Chung-kuo chin-tai ssu-hsiang-shih lun-wen chi* (Essays on modern Chinese intellectual history).

108. See Ts'ai Shang-ssu, "Lun Chang Ping-lin ssu-hsiang ti chieh-chi hsing" (On the class identity of Chang Ping-lin's ideology), [318], 1962, no. 1, pp.58-70.

109. See articles by Lo Yao-chiu, "Kuang Fu Hui hsing-chih t'an-t'ao" (A study of the nature of the Restoration Society), in *Hsia-meng ta-hsüeh hsüeh-pao: She-hui k'o-hsüeh pan,* (Amoy, 1960), no. 1; and "Kuang Fu Hui hsing-chih ti tsai

t'an-tao'' (A further study of the nature of the Restoration Society), *ibid.* 1961, no. 1.

110. See [318], 1962, no. 1.

111. For Liu Ta-nien's view, see [318], 1961, no. 5.

112. Such as Shao Hsün-cheng and Chu Chung-yü, *Chang T'ai-yen* (Chang Ping-lin), 1961; Ts'ao Hung-wen, ''Wo tui Liang Ch'i-ch'ao ho-ch'i ssu-hsiang ti k'an-fa'' (My views on the thought of Liang Ch'i-ch'ao in his last years), *Wen-hui pao,* 5 May 1961.

113. See, for example, the articles in commemoration of Sun's birth in a leading Taipai newspaper, *Hsin-sheng pao* (New Life Daily), 11 Nov. 1950 and 12 Nov. 1951. Also see Huang Ch'un-ch'ing, ''Kuo fu yü T'ai-wan'' (Sun Yat-sen and Taiwan) in [124], 43-58.

114. A good example is Yang Yün-p'ing, ''Kuo-min ko-ming yün-tung tui-yü T'ai-wan ti ying-hsiang'' (The impact of the Chinese national revolutionary movement upon Taiwan), [124], pp.55-62.

115. [169], *chüan-shou* 2 and *chüan* 9.

116. For a primary source, see [169], *chüan* 9, pp.87-96; and [57], Parts II and III, pp. 495-629.

117. The Kuomintang's Central Committee for the Compilation of Source Materials on Party History is cited in this chapter in its common English form: the ''Kuomintang Archives.''

118. Shen's review article appears in [320], Dec. 1959. In response to Shen's criticism, the publisher of [74] immediately appended to the book a long list of errata. Shen's article is still cited by scholars. See, for example, Wu Hsiang-hsiang's article in [337], no.86, pp.4-12. Another critical review, ''Kuo-fu nien-p'u ch'u-kao chih p'ing-i'' (Review of *Kuo-fu nien-p'u ch'u-kao* [A draft *nien-p'u* of Sun Yat-sen's career]) by Yü Peng-chih, was published in *Ko-ming ssu hsiang* (Revolutionary thought), vol. 8, no. 6 (June 1960).

119. [259], 6:41-160.

120. As this book [206] is mainly a reproduction of a long essay that was serialized several years ago in [305], the work does not

include those sources that have been made available in publications in more recent years.

121. This is part of the results of Shen's current research project sponsored by the Institute of Modern History, Academia Sinica, in Taiwan.

122. Shen, "Huang Yin-pai hsien-sheng nien-p'u ch'u-kao" (First draft of a *nien-p'u* of Huang Fu), serialized in [305], vol. 18, no. 1. Shen's view was later advanced and substantiated in [357], written by Huang Fu's widow.

123. [259], vol 5: 23-80.

124. [259], vol 6: 1-40.

125. [259], vol 3: 45-78.

126. [259], vol 5: 1-25.

127. For example, among the scholars who were invited to attend the Portsmouth Conference on the 1911 Revolution, three of the Chinese scholars were associated with the Academia Sinica.

128. Mary C. Wright, ed., *China in Revolution: The First Phase, 1900-1913* (New Haven, Ct., 1968), pp. 29-30.

# A Selected Bibliography on the
# 1911 Revolution

The items listed in this bibliography are selected from about a thousand titles of Chinese monographs, collected works, pamphlets, and periodicals. The criteria of selection are, first, that the item must be of some value to the historical study of the Revolution; second, that at least a copy of it is accessible to scholars outside the Chinese mainland; and, third, that it has not been superseded by a later work. While attention is paid to those compilations of documentary materials that reflect the political or ideological trends that influenced historical thinking on the Revolution, purely primary sources are excluded. To keep the bibliography within reasonable length, titles are listed for monographs and for anthologies and journals, but not for inclusions appearing within these publications.

Entries are listed alphabetically by author (and, if unauthored, by title). In the translations of titles, efforts have been made to preserve the tone or feeling of the original, but honorific forms of address are omitted (thus, "Sun Yat-sen" instead of "National Father" or "Late Party Director"). Information is given on the most readily accessible reprint. For the convenience of users of this Bibliography, the Hoover call number is provided at the end of those entries of which at least one edition is to be found in the 1970 Card Catalog of the East Asian Collection of the Hoover Institution. For entries lacking a call number, no copy is available in Hoover according to the 1970 card catalog. The page or pages on which the title appears in this book are given on the extreme right of the last line of the bibliographical entry.

[1] Ai-hsin-chüeh-lo P'u-i (Henry Pu Yi). *Wo ti ch'ien-pan-sheng* 我的前半生 (The first half of my life). 3 vols. Hong Kong, 1964. 2269/3425.2    52-53

[2] Ch'ai Te-keng *et al.,* comps. *Hsin-hai ko-ming* 辛亥革命 (The Revolution of 1911). 8 vols., Shanghai, 1956. 2960/2920    2, 50-51, 90-91, 94-96,

[3] Chang Chi. *Chang P'u-ch'üan hsien-sheng ch'üan-chi* 張溥泉先生全集 (Collected writings of Chang Chi). Taipei, 1951; and *pu-pien* 補編 (supplement), Taipei, 1951. 2269/1321    98, 129 72

[4] Chang Ch'i-yün *et al.,* eds. *Ch'ing-shih* 清史 (A history of the Ch'ing dynasty). 8 vols., Taipei, 1961. See [24] for additional bibliographic information. 2741/3528    74,107

[5] _____ . *Tang-shih kai-yao* 黨史概要 (Essentials of the [Kuomintang] party history). 5 vols. Taipei, 1951-1952. 4738.28/1346.95    90

[6] Chang Chiang-ts'ai. *Wang Ching-wei hsien-sheng keng-hsü meng-nan pieh-lu* 汪精衛先生庚戌蒙難別錄 (Anecdotal accounts of the 1910 trials and tribulations of Wang Ching-wei). Nanking, 1941. 2269/3138.13a    39

[7] _____ . *Wang Ching-wei hsien-sheng, keng-hsü meng-nan shih-lu* 汪精衛先生庚戌蒙難實錄 (A true account of the 1910 trials and tribulations of Wang Ching-wei). Peking? 1937; rev. ed., Nanking, 1940. 2260/3138.13    39

[8] Chang Ching-lu, comp. *Chung-kuo chin-tai ch'u-pan shih-liao* 中国近代出版史料 (Source materials on the history of modern Chinese publications). *Ch'u-pien* 初編 (Part I), Peking, 1953; *Erh-pein* 二編 (Part II), Peking, 1954. (This series was to evolve into a huge compilation, with its third, fourth, fifth and seventh parts published under the title of item [10] and its sixth part under the title of [9]). 9470.8/1350pt.1&2    53, 100, 105-6

[9] _____ , comp. *Chung-kuo ch'u-pan shih-liao pu-pien* 中国出版史料補編 (Supplementary materials on the history of Chinese publications). Peking, 1957. (See [8] for additional bibliographic information.) 9470.8/1350.1    100, 105

[10] _____ , comp. *Chung-kuo hsien-tai ch'u-pan shih-liao* 中国現代出版史料 (Source materials on the his-

tory of contemporary Chinese publications). Vol. 1, Peking, 1954; vol. 2, 1955; vol. 3, 1956; vol. 4, 1959 (2 *ts'e*). (See [8] for additional bibliographic information.) 9470.8/1350                100, 105

[11] Chang Hsiao-jo, comp. *Chang Chi-tzu chiu-lu* 張季子九錄 (Collected Works of Chang Ch'ien). 25 *ts'e*. Shanghai, 1931. 2269/1336

[12] _____ . *Nan-t'ung Chang Chi-chih hsien-sheng chuan-chi* 南通張季直先生傳記 (A biography of Chang Ch'ien from Nantung). Shanghai, 1929; reprint, Taipei, 1965. 2269/1336                26

[13] Chang Hsing-yen. *Su-pao an chi-shih* 蘇報案紀實 (An account of the Su Pao case). Shanghai, n.d. Taipei reprint, 1968.                90

[14] Chang K'ai-mei. *(Hsin-hai) Hsin-chiang I-li luan-shih pen-mo* (辛亥)新疆伊犁亂事本末 (The [1911] incident at Ili, Sinkiang). n.p., 1912. 2960/1374                92

[15] Chang Kuo-kan. *Hsin-hai ko-ming shih-liao* 辛亥革命史料 (Historical materials on the 1911 Revolution). Shanghai, 1958. 2960/1363

[16] Chang Nan and Wang Jen-chih, comps. *Hsin-hai ko-ming ch'ien shih-nien chien shih-lun hsüan-chi* 辛亥革命前十年間時論選集 (Selections of writings on current affairs during the decade preceding the Revolution of 1911). First *chüan*, 2 vols., Peking, 1960; reprint, Hong Kong, 1962; second *chüan*. 2 vols., Peking, 1962. 4739/1344                51

[17] Chang Nan-hsien. *Hu-pei ko-ming chih-chih lu* 湖北革命知之錄 (What we know about the Revolution in Hupeh). Chungking, 1945; reprint, Shanghai, 1946. 2962/1342   35, 97

[18] Chang P'eng-yüan. *Liang Ch'i-ch'ao yü Ch'ing-chi ko-ming* 梁啟超與清季革命 (Liang Ch'i-ch'ao and the [late] Ch'ing revolution). Taipei, 1964. 2268/3934.1                74

[19] Chang Ping-lin. *Chang-shih ts'ung-shu* 章氏叢書 (Collected works of Chang Ping-lin). 24 *ts'e*. Hangchow, 1917-19. 9119/0490

[20] _____ . *Chang-shih ts'ung-shu hsü-pien* 章氏叢書續編 (A supplement to the collected works of Chang Ping-lin). 4 *ts'e*. Peking, 1933. 9119/0490.1

[21] _____ . *T'ai-yen hsien-sheng tzu-ting nien-p'u*
太炎先生自訂年譜 (An autobiographic *nien-p'u* of
Chang Ping-lin). Mimeo., Soochow, 1928; reprinted in [291],
no. 1, Sept. 1935; reproduced in single volume with appended
biographical accounts of Chang and bibliographies of his works.
Hong Kong, 1965. 2279/0490

[22] Chang Yü-k'un. *Wen-hsüeh-she Wu-ch'ang shou-i
chi-shih* 文學社武昌首義紀實 (A factual account of
the Wuchang Uprising staged by the Society of Letters). Nanking, 1944; rev. ed., Peking, 1955. 2962/0436 & 2962/0436a       37

[23] Chang Yung-fu. *Nan-yang yü ch'uang-li Min-kuo*
南洋與創立民國 (Southeast Asia and the founding of
the Republic). Shanghai, 1933. 2960/1333

[24] Chao Erh-hsün *et al.*, comps. *Ch'ing-shih-kao* 清
史稿 (A draft history of the Ch'ing dynasty). Peking, 1927.
536 *chüan*, 131 vols. 2741/4817

For a conveniently available English summary of the bibliographical information, see Thurston Griggs, "The Ch'ing
Shih Kao: A Bibliographical Summary," *Harvard Journal of
Asiatic Studies* vol. 18, nos. 1-2 (June 1955): 105-23. Of all
the editions, the Mukden edition of 1937 (in 529 *chüan*) has
been most accessible and was recently photo-reproduced in two
volumes in Hong Kong. Most parts of this work have been       26, 33,
reproduced in [4].                                            74, 97

[25] *Ch'en Ching-ts'un hsien-sheng nien-p'u* 陳競存
先生年譜 (A *nien-p'u* of Ch'en Chiung-ming). Hong
Kong? 1950? (2269/7996.1)

[26] Ch'en Hsi-ch'i. *T'ung-meng-hui ch'eng-li ch'ien ti
Sun Chung-shan* 同盟會成立前的孫中山 (SunYat-
sen [in the years] preceding the founding of the Tung Meng
Hui). Canton, 1957. 4738.31/1904.52

[27] Ch'en Hsiung. *Huang-hua-kang ko-ming lieh-shih
chuan* 黃花岡革命烈士傳 (Biographies of the revolutionary martyrs on Yellow Flower Hill). Taipei, 1957. 2261/4474.1

[28] Ch'en Hsü-lu. *Hsin-hai ko-ming* 辛亥革命
(The Revolution of 1911). Shanghai, 1955. 2960/7944       90, 100

[29] _____ . *Tsou Jung yü Ch'en T'ien-hua ti ssu-*

*hsiang* 鄒容與陳天華的思想   (The thought of Tsou Jung and Ch'en Tien-hua). Shanghai, 1957. 2259.9/7944

[30] Ch'en Ku-t'ing. *Kuo-fu yü Jih-pen yu-jen* 國父與日本友人 (Sun Yat-sen and his Japanese friends). Taipei, 1965. In the series of *Kuo-fu pai-nien tan-ch'en chi-nien ts'ung-k'an* 國父百年誕辰紀念叢刊 (Collected works commemorating the centenary of Sun Yat-sen's birth). 4738.31/1904.71

69

[31] Ch'en Kung-fu. *Chung-kuo tsui-chin san-shih-nien shih* 中國最近三十年史 (A history of China during the past thirty years). Shanghai, 1928. 2970/7915

[32] Ch'en Po-ta. *Ch'ieh-kuo ta-tao Yüan Shih-k'ai* 竊國大盜袁世凱 (The great usurper Yüan Shih-k'ai). Peking, 1955, See [33] for additional bibliographic information. 2269/4342c

49, 108

[33] _____ . *Chieh-shao ch'ieh-kuo ta-tao Yüan Shih-k'ai* 介紹竊國大盜袁世凱 (An introduction to Yüan Shih-k'ai, the usurper). First published as an article in *Ch'ün-chung* (The Masses), 10:23 (Dec. 1945). Reproduced in single volumes, Yenan, 1946; Kalgan, 1946; see also [32] and [79] for the text reproduced under different titles. 2269/4342a

49, 108

[34] Ch'en Shao-pai. *Hsing-chung-hui ko-ming shih-yao* 興中會革命史要 (Essentials of the revolutionary history of the Hsing Chung Hui). First published in [288], 1929-30; later in a single volume, Nanking, 1935; reprint, Taipei, 1956. 4738.31/1904.58

27, 91

[35] Cheng Chao *et al*. *Sun Chung-san hsien-sheng kan-i-lu* 孫中山先生感憶錄 (Reminiscent accounts on Sun Yat-sen). Taipei, 1965. 4738.31/1904.352

[36] [Cheng Lieh] T'ien-hsiao-sheng, pseud. *Huang-hua-kang Fu-chien shih-chieh chi-shih* 黃花岡福建十傑紀實 (Ten Fukienese [revolutionary] martyrs on the Yellow Flower-Hill). N.p., 1912. Reprinted in [186].

92

[37] Cheng Lieh. *Lin ta-chiang-chün chuan* 林大將軍傳 (A biography of Lin Wen, the great [revolutionary] soldier). Taipei, 1953. Bound together with another work of the same author, *Li-tai jen-wu p'ing-yung* 历代人物評詠 (Poems on historical figures). 2261/8213

[38] Chiang Hsing-te. *Kuo-fu Sun Chung-shan hsien-sheng chuan* 國父孫中山先生傳 (A biography of Sun Yat-sen, the father of the Republic). Shanghai, 1945; reprint, Taipei, 1950. 4738.31/1904

[39] Chiang Tso-pin. *Chiang Yü-yen hsien-sheng tzu-chuan* 蔣雨岩先生自傳 (Autobiography of Chiang Tso-pin). Chungking, 1943. Reprinted as *Chiang Tso-pin hui-i-lu* 蔣作賓回憶錄 (Memoirs of Chiang Tso-pin). Taipei, 1967. 2269/4423.42

[40] Ch'ien Chi-po. *Hsin-hai nan-pei i-ho pieh-chi* 辛亥南北議和別記 (Supplementary notes to the account of the 1911 North-South negotiations). Chinkiang, 1928.

[41] Ch'ien Hsing-ts'un (alias Ah Ying and Chang Yü-ying), comp. *Wan-Ch'ing hsi-chü hsiao-shuo shu-mu* 晚清戲劇小說書目 (A bibliography of plays and fiction of the late Ch'ing period). Shanghai, 1954. 5738.8/8544    100

[42] ———. *Wan-Ch'ing hsiao-shuo shih* 晚清小說史 (A history of late Ch'ing fiction). Shanghai, 1937. 5733.8/8544    100

[43] ———. *Wan-Ch'ing wen-i pao-k'an shu-lüeh* 晚清文藝報刊述畧 (A digest of the literary journals of the late Ch'ing period). Shanghai, 1956. 9971/8544    100

[44] Chih-yin-sheng, pseud., comp. *O-luan hui-lu ch'u-pien* 鄂亂彙錄初編 (Collected materials relating to the Hupeh rebellion, part one). N.p., 1911. 2962/4372    92

[45] Chin Yü-fu, comp. *Hsüan-t'ung cheng-chi* 宣統政紀 (Official documents of the Hsüan-t'ung period). 16 *ts'e*. Dairen, 1934. 2940/3212

[46] Ching-shih wen-she, ed. *Min-kuo ching-shih wen-pien* 民國經世文編 (Collected essays on current affairs in the Republican period). 40 *ts'e*. Shanghai, 1914; reprint in 4 vols., Taipei, 1962. 4603/2403

[47] Chou K'ai-ch'ing. *Ssu-ch'uan yü hsin-hai ko-ming* 四川與辛亥革命 (Szechwan and the 1911 Revolution). Taipei, 1964. 2960/7270    70

[48] Chou Shan-p'ei. *Hsin-hai Ssu-ch'uan shih-pien chih wo* 辛亥四川事變之我 (My position during the 1911 incident of Szechwan). Chungking, 1938.

37

[49] ———. *Hsin-hai Ssu-ch'uan cheng-lu ch'in-li chi* 辛亥四川爭路親歷記 (Reminiscences on the railway disputes of 1911 in Szechwan). Chungking, 1957. 4500/7284

[50] Chu Hsin-fan. *Chung-kuo ko-ming yü Chung-kuo she-hui ko chieh-chi* 中國革命與中國社會各階級 (The Chinese revolution and the social classes in China). 2 vols. Shanghai, 1930. 4130.9/2944

45

[51] Chu Te-shang. *Liu K'uei-i* 劉揆一 ([The life of] Lui K'uei-i). N.p., 1912. 2269/7251

[52] Chu Wen-ping. *Shang-hai kuang-fu chu-chih-ts'u* 上海光復竹枝詞 (Poems on the restoration of Shang-hai [from Manchu rule]). Shanghai, n.d.

[53] Chü Cheng. *Mei-ch'uan jih-chi* 梅川日記 (Reminiscences of Chü Cheng). Chungking, 1945. Included in [54] and [55]. 2269/7611.1

37, 97

[54] ———. *Hsin-hai cha-chi Mei-ch'uan jih-chi ho-k'an* 辛亥劄記梅川日記合刊 (Notes on the 1911 [Revolution] *and* Reminiscences of Chü Cheng). Taipei, 1956. 2960/7611

110

[55] ———. *Chü Chüeh-sheng hsien-sheng ch'üan-chi* 居覺生先生全集 (Collected works of Chü Cheng). 2 vols. Taipei, 1954. 2269/7611

72, 93, 97, 110

[56] Ch'ü Ch'iu-pai. *Chung-kuo ko-ming chih cheng-lun wen-t'i* 中國革命之爭論問題 (The controversial issues concerning the Chinese revolution). N.p., 1927; 1928. 4929.1/6122

99

[57] Chung-hua min-kuo k'ai-kuo wu-shih-nien wen-hsien pien-tsuan wei-yüan-hui, comp. *Chung-hua-min-kuo k'ai-kuo wu-shih-nien wen-hsien* 中華民國開國五十年文獻 (A documentary collection in celebration of the Jubilee of the founding of the Republic of China). Taipei. Since 1961 twenty-one volumes have appeared: Part I, vols. 1-2, *Ko-ming yüan-yüan* 革命遠源 (The origin of the Revolution); vols. 3-6, *Lieh-ch'iang chin-lüeh* 列強侵

罢(Encroachment of foreign powers); vols. 7-8, *Ch'ing-t'ing chih kai-ko yü fan-tung* 清廷之改革與反動(Reforms and reactionary measures of the Manchu court); vols. 9-10, *Ko-ming chih ch'ang-tao yü fa-chan: Hsing-chung-hui* 革命之倡導的發展:興中會(The advocacy and development of the Revolution: the Revive China Society); vols. 11-16, *Ko-ming chih ch'ang-tao yü fa-chan : Chung-kuo T'ung-meng-hui* 革命之倡導的發展:中國同盟會 (The advocacy and development of the Revolution: the United League of China); Part II, vol. 1, *Wu-ch'ang shou-i* 武昌首義 (The Wuchang Uprising); vol. 2, *K'ai-kuo kuei-mu* 開國規模 (The founding of the Republic); vols. 3-5, *Ko-sheng kuang-fu* 各省光復 (The restoration of the provinces). 2970/5476      66-67, 74,102 140

[58] Chung-hua min-kuo ko-chieh chi-nien kuo-fu pai-nien tan-ch'en ch'ou-pei wei-yüan-hui, ed. *Ko-ming hsien-lieh hsien-chin ch'an-yang kuo-fu ssu-hsiang lun-wen-chi* 革命先烈先進闡揚國父思想論文集 (Collected essays of revolutionary martyrs and pioneers in exposition of the thought of Sun Yat-sen). 3 vols. Taipei, 1965. 4738.12/5476.68

[59] _____ , ed. *Ko-ming hsien-lieh hsien-chin chuan* 革命先烈先進傳 (Biographical writings of the martyrs and pioneers in the revolutionary movement). Taipei, 1965. 4738.31/5667.48      71

[60] _____ , ed. *Kuo-fu pai-nien tan-ch'en chi-nien lun-wen-chi* 國父百年誕辰紀念論文集 (Collected essays in commemoration of the centenary of Sun Yat-sen's birth). 5 vols. Taipei, 1965. 4738.12/0432      68

[61] Chung-kuo hsien-tai-shih yen-chiu hui, ed. *Chung-kuo hsien-tai ko-ming yün-tung shih* 中國現代革命運動史(A history of the revolutionary movement in contemporary China). N.p., 1938; n.p., 1940; Yenan, 1941. 2744/5612a      100

[62] Chung-kuo hsien-tai-shih yen-chiu wei-yüan hui, ed. *Chung-kuo hsien-tai ko-ming yün-tung shih* 中國現代革命運動史(A history of the revolutionary movement in contemporary China). N.p., 1937; reprint, Hong Kong, 1949. 2744/5612 & 2744/5612b

[63] Chung-kuo jen-min cheng-chih hsieh-shang hui-i.
Ch'üan-kuo wei-yüan-hui. Wen-shih tzu-liao yen-chiu wei-
yüan-hui, ed. *Hsin-hai ko-ming hui-i-lu* 辛亥革命回憶
錄 (Recollections on the Revolution of 1911). 5 vols.
Peking, 1961-63. 2960/5687.04                                         52

[64] Chung-kuo jen-min cheng-chih hsieh-shang hui-
i. Hu-pei sheng wei-yüan-hui, ed. *Hsin-hai shou-i hui-i-lu*
辛亥首義回憶錄(Recollections on the first [Wuchang]
uprising in 1911). 2 vols. Hankow, 1957. 2960/5687          52

[65] Chung-kuo k'o-hsüeh-yüan. Chin-tai-shih yen-
chiu-so, ed. *Hsin-hai ko-ming tzu-liao* 辛亥革命資料
(Source materials on the 1911 Revolution). Peking, 1961.
A special issue (no. 25) of *Chin-tai-shih tzu-liao*近代史
資料(see [292]): 2748/3253                                            51

[66] Chung-kuo k'o-hsüeh-yüan. Li-shih yen-chiu-so.
ed. *Yün-nan Kuei-chou hsin-hai ko-ming tzu-liao*雲南貴州
辛亥革命資料    (Materials on the 1911 Revolu-
tion in Yunnan and Kweichow). Peking, 1959. 2960/5627       100

[67] Chung-kuo k'o-hsüeh-yüan. Li-shih yen-chiu-so
*and* Pei-ching ta-hsüeh. Li-shih-hsi, eds. *Chung-kuo shih-
hsüeh lun-wen so-yin*中國史學論文索引 (Index to
Chinese historical articles). 2 vols. Peking, 1957. 9559/5627   100

[68] Chung-kuo kuo-min-tang. Chung-yang chih-hsing
wei-yüan-hui. Hsi-nan chih-hsing-pu. Hsüan-ch'uan-tsu, ed.
*Ko-ming hsien-lieh chi-nien chuan-k'an* 革命先烈紀念
專刊 (A special anthology in commemoration of revolutionary martyrs). Canton, 1932. 2961/5667                     29, 95

[69] Chung-kuo kuo-min-tang. Chung-yang chih-hsing
wei-yüan-hui. Ko-ming chai-wu tiao-ch'a wei-yüan-hui, ed.
*Ko-ming chai-chüan chung-lui piao*革命債券種類表
(A tabulation of the "Revolution Bonds"). Nanking, 1935.
2960/5667, microfilm

[70] Chung-kuo kuo-min-tang. Chung-yang hsüan-
ch'uan-pu, ed. *Kuo-fu Sun hsien-sheng nien-p'u* 國父孫
先生年譜(A *nien-p'u* of Mr. Sun, Father of the Republic). Chungking, 1940. 4738.31/1904.25

[71] Chung-kuo kuo-min-tang. Chung-yang tang-shih
shih-liao pien-tsuan wei-yüan-hui, comp. *Chung-kuo kuo-*

*min-tang wu-shih chou-nien chi-nien t'e-k'an* 中國國民黨
五十周年紀念特刊 (A special anthology in celebration of the Jubilee of the Kuomintang.). Chungking, 1944.
4738.28/5667.1                                                      98

[72] _____ . _____, *Ko-ming hsien-lieh chan-chi*
(Biographies of revolutionary martyrs).
Chungking, 1944. 4738.31/0323.1

[73] _____ . _____ , ed. *Ko-ming wen-hsien*   2, 66,
革 命 文 獻 (Documents on the Revolution). Taipei.   71, 96,
57 vols. have appeared since 1953. 2970/6132               98

[74] _____ . _____, ed. *Kuo-fu nien-p'u* 國父
年譜 (A *nien-p'u* of Sun Yat-sen's career). Taipei, 1958;   70-71,
rev. and enl. ed., 2 vols., Taipei, 1969. 4738.31/1904.241   123

[75] _____ . _____, ed. *Liu-shih-nien lai chih
Chung-kuo kuo-min-tang yü Chung-kuo* 六十年來之中
國國民黨與中國 (The Kuomintang and China
during the past sixty years). Taipei, 1954. 4738.28/6132

[76] _____ . _____ . ed. *Tsung-li nien-p'u
ch'ang-pien ch'u-kao* 總理年譜長編初稿 (First
draft of a detailed *nien-p'u* of Sun Yat-sen). Nanking, 1932.
4738.31/1904.24                                                     95

[77] Chung-kuo kuo-min-tang. Kuang-tung-sheng chih-
hsing wei-yüan-hui, ed. *Tsung-li tan-ch'en chinien chuan-k'an*
總理誕辰紀念專刊 (An anthology
commemorating the birthday of Sun Yat-sen). Canton, 1932.
4738.31/1904.48                                                     95

[78] Chung-yang yen-chiu yüan. Chin-tai-shih yen-chiu-so,
ed. *Chung-kuo hsien-tai-shih tzu-liao tiao-ch'a mu-lu*
中國現代史資料調查目錄 (An inventory
of source materials [in Taiwan] on contemporary Chinese his
tory). 11 vols. Taipei, 1969. 2514/0212                            77

[79] Fan Wen-lan and Ch'en Po-ta. *Tseng Kuo-fan
yü Yüan Shih-k'ai* 曾國藩與袁世凱([The life of]
Tseng Kuo-fan and of Yüan Shih-k'ai). Hankow? 1946.
2268/8664.3                                                     49, 108

[80] Feng-kang chi-men-ti-tzu, pseud., comp. *San-*

*shui Liang Yen-sun hsien-sheng nien-p'u* 三水梁燕孫先
生年譜 (A *nien-p'u* of Liang Shih-i). 2 vols. n.p.,
1939; reprint, 1946; reprint in Taipei as [234], 1962. 2269/3940f   33, 129

[81] Feng Shu. *Keng-tzu hsin-hai chung-lieh hsiang-
tsan* 庚子辛亥忠烈像贊 (Captions for the por-
traits of the loyal and martyred officials during the incidents of 1900 and 1911). 2 *ts'e*. N.p., 1934. 2259.89/3243f

[82] Feng Tzu-yu. *Chung-hua min-kuo k'ai-kuo ch'ien
ko-ming shih* 中華民國開國前革命史 (A his-
tory of the revolution [-ary movement] preceding the founding of the Republic of China). Vol. I, Shanghai. 1928; vol. II,
1930. Reprint as I, II and III, Chungking, 1944; Shanghai, 1946.
Reprint, in 2 vols., Taipei, 1954. *Hsü-pien*                          27,37,
(Supplement), Shanghai, 1946. 2960/3225.1                             92, 95,
                                                                      98

[83] ———— . *Chung-kuo ko-ming yün-tung erh-shih-
liu-nien tsu-chih shih* 中國革命運動二十六年組
織史(A history of the organizations of the Chinese revolutionary movement, 1885-1911). Shanghai, 1948. 2960/
3225.4                                                                37

[84] ———— . *Hua-ch'iao ko-ming k'ai-kuo shih* 華僑
革命開國史 (The [role of] overseas Chinese in
the history of the Revolution and of the founding of the Republic). Chungking, 1946; Shanghai, 1947; Taipei, 1953.
2960/3225.2                                                           37

[85] ———— . *Hua-ch'iao ko-ming tsu-chih shih-hua*
華僑革命組織史話(A history of the revolution-
ary organizations among the overseas Chinese). Taipei,
1954. 2960/3225.3

[86] ———— . *Ko-ming i-shih* 革命逸史 (Anec-
dotes of the Revolution). 5 vols. Vol. I, Shanghai, 1939;
vol. II, Chungking, 1943; vol. III, Chungking, 1945; vol.     37-38,
IV, Shanghai, 1945; vol. V, Shanghai, 1946; reprint, Taipei,    92,
1969. 2960/3225                                                95-96

[87] Feng Yü-hsiang. *Wo ti sheng-huo* 我的生活
(My life). Shanghai and Chungking, 1947. 2269/3213a

[88] Fu Ch'i-hsüeh. *Kuo-fu Sun Chung-shan hsien-*

*sheng chuan* 國父孫中山先生傳 (A biography
of Sun Yat-sen, the father of the Republic). Taipei, 1965.
4738.31/1904.44                                          71

[89] Han-jen, pseud. *T'ai-wan ko-ming shih* 台灣革
命史 (A history of the revolutionary [movement] in Taiwan).
Nanking, 1925; reprint, Tainan, 1945. 3071.1/3380        65

[90] Hirayama Shu. *Chung-kuo mi-mi she-hui shih*
中國秘密社會史 (A history of Chinese secret so-
cieties). Tr. from the Japanese by Shang-wu ying-shu-kuan,
pien-i-so. Shanghai, 1912; rev. ed. 1934. 4181/1427

[91] Ho Ch'i-fang. *Wu Yü-chang t'ung-chih ko-ming
ku-shih* 吳玉章同志革命故事 (The revolutionary
story of comrade Wu Yü-chang). Hong Kong, 1949 (probably a
reprint). 4292.3/2310

[92] Ho Chung-hsiao. *Ch'en Ying-shih hsien-sheng chi-
nien ch'üan-chi* 陳英士先生紀念全集 (An an-
thology in commemoration of Ch'en Ch'i-mei). 2 vols.
Shanghai, 1930. Reprint, Shanghai, 1946; Taipei, 1970.   95-96,
4738.31/7948.1                                           115

[93] _____ . *Ch'en Ying-shih hsien-sheng nien-p'u*
陳英士先生年譜 (A *nien-p'u* of Ch'en Ch'i-mei).
Included in [92] and later reproduced in a single volume.
Shanghai, 1946. 4738.31/7948

[94] Ho Hsiang-ning. *Hui-i Sun Chung-shan ho Liao
Chung-k'ai* 回憶孫中山和廖仲愷 (Reminiscences
on Sun Yat-sen and Liao Chung-k'ai). Peking, 1957.
4738.31/1904.54                                          52

[95] Ho Po-yen. *Chu Chih-hsin, Liao Chung-k'ai* 朱
執信,廖仲愷([The life of] Chu Chih-hsin and of Liao
Chung-k'ai). Nanking, 1946. 4738.31/2942

[96] _____ . *Huang K'o-ch'iang* 黃克強
([The life of] Huang Hsing). Nanking, 1946. 4738.31/4878

[97] _____ . *Lu Hao-tung, Shih Chien-ju* 陸皓東
史劍如([The life of] Lu Hao-tung and of Shih Chien-ju).
Nanking, 1946. 4738.31/7154

[98] Hsi Yün-chang. *Ch'i-shih-erh lieh-shih chung ti
hua-ch'iao* 七十二烈士中的華僑 (The revolution-
aries of overseas Chinese origin among the seventy-two

martyrs [of the "March 29" incident]). Taipei, 1958. 2961/
6110

[99] _____ . *Ko-ming hsien-lieh shih-lüeh* 革命先
烈史畧 (Biographies of revolutionary martyrs). Taipei,
1957. 4738.31/6110

[100] Hsia-an nien-p'u hui-kao pien-ying hui, ed. *Yeh
Hsia-an hsien-sheng nien-p'u* 葉遐菴先生年譜(A *nien-
p'u* of Yeh Kung-ch'o). N.p., 1946. 2279/4942

[101] Hsiang-hai chien-k'o, pseud., ed. *Ko-ming tsung-t'ung
Li Yüan-hung hsiao-shih* 革命總統黎元洪小史
(A brief history of [the career of] the revolutionary president Li
Yüan-hung). Canton, 1911. 2269/2313.1                        92

[102] Hsiao I-shan. *Ch'ing-tai t'ung-shih* 清代通史
(A history of the Ch'ing dynasty). Rev. and enl. ed. 5 vols.
Taipei, 1963. 2744/4212.2

[103] Hsieh Pin. *Min-kuo cheng-tang shih* 民國政
黨史 (A history of political parties in the Republican
period). Shanghai, 1927; reprint, Taipei, 1962. 4737/0442

[104] Hsien Chiang. *Yu Lieh shih-lüeh* 尤列事
畧(The life of Yu Lieh). Hong Kong, 1951. 4738.31/4112

[105] *Hsin-ch'ing-nien* she, ed. *Chung-kuo ko-ming
wen-t'i lun-wen chi* 中國革命問題論文集 (Es-
says on the problem of revolution in China). Canton?
1926. 4292.1/0583                                           99

[106] Hsü Chih-jen. *Sun I-hsien chuan-chi* 孫逸仙傳
記 (A biography of Sun Yat-sen). Shanghai, 1926; 1946.
An abridged version, Shanghai, 1927; Chungking, 1941 [A
translation from *A Biography of Sun Yat-sen* by Paul
Myron Wentworth Linebarger]. 4738.31/1904.la

[107] Hsü Hsüeh-erh *et al. Sung Yü-fu* 宋漁父
([The life of] Sung Chiao-jen). Shanghai, 1913. Reprinted as
[279]. 2980/3942.2                                         133

[108] Hsü Hu-lin , ed. Hsin-hai hsün-nan chi
(Martyrdom of 1911). N.p., n.d. 辛亥殉難記

[109] Hsü Shih-shen. *Kuo-fu hsüan-jen lin-shih ta-tsung-t'ung
shih-lu* 國父選任臨時大總統實錄
(A true account of the election of Sun Yat-sen to the provisional
presidency). Nanking, 1948; reprint with slight change in title, 2
vols., Taipei, 1967. 2971/0429

[110] _____ . *Kuo-fu ko-ming yüan-ch'i hsiang-chu* 國父革命緣起詳註 (Detailed annotations to [210], Sun Yat-sen's *Ko-ming yüan-ch'i* [The origin of the Revolution]). Shanghai, 1947; reprint, Taipei, 1954. 4738.31/1904.35          38, 126

[111] Hsü Shih-yin. *Mien-tien Chung-kuo T'ung-meng-hui k'ai-kuo ko-ming shih* (The revolutionary history of the Burma branch of the Tung Meng Hui). 2 vols. Rangoon, 1931? Vol. I, 4738.29/2907

[112] *Hsün-huan jih-pao*, ed. *Kuang-tung ko-tang ch'i-shih chi* 廣東各黨起事記 (The ["March 29th"] revolutionary upring in Knangtung). Hong Kong, 1911. 4738.29/0549

[113] Hu Ch'ü-fei. *Sun Chung-shan hsien-sheng chuan* 孫中山先生傳 (A biography of Sun Yat-sen). Shanghai, 1930; reprint, Changsha, 1939. 4738.31/1904.15          27

[114] _____ . *Tsung-li shih-lüeh* 總理事署 (The career of Sun Yat-sen). Shanghai, 1937. 4738.31/1904.151

[115] Hu-nan wen-hsien wei-yüan-hui, comp. *Hu-nan wen-hsien hui-pien* 湖南文獻彙編 (A collection of documents concerning Hunan province). Changsha, 1948.          37

[116] Hu O-kung. *Hsin-hai ko-ming pei-fang shih-lu* 辛亥革命北方實錄 (A factual account of the revolution in North China). Shanghai, 1948. Reprint, Taipei, 1970. 2960/4268

[117] Hu-pei che-hsüeh she-hui k'o-hsüeh lien-ho-hui, ed. *Hsin-hai ko-ming wu-shih chou-nien lun-wen-chi* 辛亥革命五十週年論文集 (An anthology in celebration of the Jubilee of the 1911 Revolution). Hankow, 1962. 2960/3195          37, 97          101

[118] Hu Sheng. *Sun Chung-shan ko-ming fen-to hsiao-shih* 孫中山革命奮鬥小史 (A brief account of the revolutionary struggles of Sun Yat-sen). Hong Kong, 1948. 4738.31/1904.11          50

[119] _____ . *Ti-kuo-chu-i yü Chung-kuo cheng-chih* 帝國主義與中國政治 (Imperialism and Chinese politics). Hong Kong, 1948; rev. ed., Peking, 1952; 2nd rev. ed., Peking, 1954. 2488/4221          49

[120] Hu Tsu-shun. *Liu-shih t'an-wang* 歷史談往 (Reminiscences at sixty). Chungking, 1944. 2269/4232

[121] _____ . *Wu-ch'ang k'ai-kuo shih-lu* 武昌開 97
國賓錄(A factual account of the founding of the Republic in Wuchang). 2 vols. Wuchang, 1948. 2960/4232    97

[122] Hua Kang. *Chung-hua min-tsu chieh-fang yün-tung shih* 中華民族解放運動史 (A history of the Chinese people's liberation movement). 2 vols. Chungking? 1940. Chungking and Hong Kong, 1947 and 1948; Shanghai, 1948. The second volume is largely a reproduction of [123]. 2744/4522    46, 99

[123] _____    *I-chiu erh-wu chih i-chiu erh-ch'i ti Chung-kuo ta-ko-ming shih* 一九二五至一九二七的中 國大革命史 (The great revolution in China, 1925-27).    45-46, Shanghai, 1931. 2982/4522    118

[124] Huang Ch'ao-ch'in. *Kuo-min ko-ming yün-tung yü T'ai-wan* 國民革命運動與台灣(The National Revolution and Taiwan). Taipei, 1955. 3071.1/4841    102

[125] Huang Fu-luan. *Hua-ch'iao yü Chung-kuo ko-ming* 華僑與中國革命(Overseas Chinese and the Chinese revolution). Hong Kong, 1954. 2960/4832

[126] Huang Hung-shou. *Ch'ing-shih chi-shih-pen-mo* 清史紀事本末(A full account of the Ch'ing dynasty). 8 *ts'e*. Shanghai, 1915. 2743/4834

[127] Huang I, ed. *Yüan-shih tao-kuo chi* 袁氏盜國 記(An account of Yüan Shih-k'ai's usurpation). Hong Kong? 1916?; reprint, Taipei, 1962. 2269/4342.14a

[128] Huang San-te. *Hung-meng ko-ming shih* 洪門 革命史  (The revolutionary history of the Triad secret society). San Francisco? 1936. 2960/4812

[129] Huang Yin-pai hsien-sheng chi-nien-k'an pien-chi wei-yüan-hui, ed. *Huang Ying-pai hsien-sheng ku-chiu kan-i-lu* 黃膺白先生故舊感憶錄(Reminiscences on Huang Fu by his friends). Shanghai, 1937; reprint, Taipei, 1962. 2269/4822

[130] [Ike Lyokichi] Tuan-shui-lou chu-jen, pseud. *Chung-kuo ko-ming shih-ti chien-wen lu* 中國革命實地 見聞錄(An eyewitness account of the Chinese revolution). Shanghai, 1927; reprint, Taipei, 1968. Tr. by Yüeh Ssu-ping from *Shina Kakumei jiken* (first serialized in *Asahi shimbun*, May-June 1908; reprinted as a separate volume, Tokyo, 1911). 2960/2140

[131] Jung Meng-yüan. *Chung-kuo chin-pai-nien ko-ming shih-lüeh* 中國近百年革命史畧 (A brief account of Chinese revolution during the past century). Peking, 1954. 2744/9913

[132] Kao Lao. *Hsin-hai ko-ming shih* 辛亥革命史 (A history of the Revolution of 1911). Reprint of a serialized article from [336]. Shanghai, 1923; Taipei reprint, 1967. 2960/0292

[133] Kao Liang-tso. *Sun Chung-shan hsien-sheng chuan* 孫中山先生傳 (A biography of Sun Yat-sen). Chungking, 1945.

[134] Kao Nai-t'ung, comp. *Ts'ai Chieh-min hsien-sheng chuan-lüeh* 蔡孑民先生傳畧 (Biographical accounts of Ts'ai Yüan-p'ei). Chungking, 1943.

[135] Kao Shao-hsien. *Hsin-hai ko-ming* 辛亥革命 (The Revolution of 1911). Shanghai, 1950. 2963/0202

[136] Ko Kung-chen. *Chung-kuo pao-hsüeh shih* 中國報學史 (A history of journalism in China). Shanghai, 1926?; reprint, Peking, 1955. 4660.9/1084

[137] Ko-ming chi-nien hui, ed. *Huang-hua-kang ch'i-shih-erh-lieh-shih shih-lüeh* 黃花岡七十二烈士事略 (Biographical accounts of the seventy-two martyrs on Yellow-Flower Hill). Canton, 1922. For rev. and enl. version see [138]. 20

[138] _____ , ed. *Kuang-chou san-yüeh erh-shih-chiu ko-ming-shih* 廣州三月二十九革命史 (A history of the "March 29" uprising in Canton). Shanghai, 1926. Reprinted as [240]. 2961/2226.1a 94, 119, 129

[139] Ku Chung-hsiu. *Chung-hua min-kuo k'ai-kuo shih* 中華民國開國史 (A history of the founding of the Republic of China). First publ. in the Shanghai journal *Cheng-i tsa-chih,* 1914; separately reprinted in Shanghai, 1917 and 1926; in Taipei, 1962. 2970/8682 21

[140] Kuang-chou hsien-tao she, ed. *Ko-ming hsien-lieh chi* 革命先烈記 (Collected writings on revolutionary martyrs). Canton, 1935. 4738.31/0323

[141] Kuang-tung wen-hsien-kuan, ed. *Kuang-tung wen-wu t'e-chi* 廣東文物特輯 (A special collection of materials relating to Kwangtung). Canton, 1948. 3073/0502 97

[142] K'ung Keng. *Hsien-lieh Wu Lu-chen hsün-nan chi* 先烈吳祿貞殉難記(The martyrdom of Wu Lu-chen). Manuscript, 1943. 4738.31/2332

[143] Kuo Chan-po. *Chin wu-shih-nien Chung-kuo ssu-hsiang-shih* 近五十年中國思想史 (An intellectual history of China during the past fifty years). Peiping, 1936; reprint, Hong Kong, 1965. 1030/0233

[144] Kuo-fang-pu, Shih-cheng-chü. *K'ai-kuo chan-shih* (A military history of the founding of the Republic). Taipei, 1966. 2260.8/6710

[145] Kuo Hsiao-ch'eng. *Chung-kuo ko-ming chi-shih-pen-mo* 中國革命紀事本末 (A full account of the Chinese Revolution). Shanghai, 1912. 2961/6720                16, 97

[146] Kuo-min pien-i she, ed. *Huang-hua-kang lieh-shih hsün-nan chi* 黃花岡烈士殉難記 (The martyrdom of revolutionaries buried at Yellow Flower Hill). N.p, 1927. 2961/6720                90, 100

[147] Kuo Mo-jo *et al.*, eds. *Chung-kuo shih-kao* (A draft history of China). Vol. 4, Peking, 1962. 2510/0234 中國史考

[148] _____ . *Mo-jo wen-chi* 沫若文存 (Collected works of Kuo Mo-jo). 17 vols. Peking, 1957. 5768/0234.021                99, 120

[149] _____ . *Shao-nien shih-tai* 少年時代 (My youth). Shanghai, 1948; reprinted in [148]. 2269/0234

[150] Kuo-shih hsin-wen she, ed. *Pei-ching ping-pien shih-mo chi* 北京兵變始末記(A full account of the mutiny in Peking). Peking, 1912; reprint, Taipei, 1962. 2975/6507

[151] Kuo T'ing-i. *T'ai-wan shih-shih kai-shuo* 台灣史事概説(An outline history of Taiwan). Taipei, 1954. 3071.1/0212                65

[152] Li Chien-nung. *Chung-kuo chin-pai-nien cheng-chih-shih* 中國近百年政治史 (A political history of modern China: 1840-1928). 2 vols. Shanghai, 1947. Reprint, Taipei, 1956. The parts on Sun Yat-sen and on the revolutionary movement are largely adapted from an earlier work of the author [153]. (Abridged English trans., by S.Y. Teng and J. Ingalls, publ. under the title of *The*

*Political History of China, 1840-1928.* Princeton, 1950.)
2744/4485                                                              93-95

[153] _____ . *Tsui-chin san-shih-nien Chung-kuo
cheng-chih-shih* 最近三十年中國政治史 (A
political history of modern China during the past thirty   26, 92,
years). Shanghai, 1930, 1933. 2970/4485                     94, 120

[154] Li Chu-jan. *Hsin-hai ko-ming ch'ien ti ch'ün-
chung tou-cheng* 辛亥革命前的羣眾斗爭 (The
mass struggles preceding the 1911 Revolution). Peking, 1957.
2960/4482

[155] Li Hsü. *Ts'ai Sung-p'o* 蔡松坡 (The life
of Ts'ai O). Nanking, 1946. 4738.31/4982

[156] Li Hung-ju. *Kuo-fu yü Chiang-su* 國父與江
蘇(Sun Yat-sen and Kiangsu). 2 vols. Taipei, 1965. 3069/
4432                                                                    70

[157] Li Keng-yüan . *Hsüeh-sheng nien-lu* 雪生
年錄 (The autobiography of Li Keng-yüan). N.p. 1934;
reprint, Taipei, 1966. 2744/3256.15

[158] Li Lieh-chün. *Li Lieh-chün tzu-chuan* 李烈鈞
自傳 (The autobiography of Li Lieh-chün). N.p., 1934;
reprint, Taipei, 1961. 2269/4418

[159] Li Lien-fang. *Hsin-hai Wu-ch'ang shou-i chi* 辛亥
武昌首義記(The Wuchang Uprising of 1911). Wu-
chang, 1949; reprint, Taipei, 1969. 2 vols. 2960/4400    37, 97

[160] Li Liu-ju. *Liu-shih-nien ti pien-ch'ien* 六十年
的變遷([An eyewitness account of] changes [in China]
during the past sixty years). Vol. 1, Peking, 1959. 5769/
4404

[161] Li P'ing-shu. *Ch'ieh-huan ch'i-shih-sui tzu-hsü*
且頑七十歲自敍 (The autobiography of Li P'ing-
shu). Shanghai, 1922. 4 *ts'e.*

[162] Li Shi-yüeh. *Hsin-hai ko-ming shih-ch'i Liang-
Hu ti-ch'ü ti ko-ming yün-tung* 辛亥革命时期兩湖
地區的革命運動(The revolutionary movements in
Hupeh and Hunan during the period of the 1911 Revolution).
Peking, 1957. 2960/4467                                               92

[163] [Li Shu] Li Nai-han. *Hsin-hai ko-ming ch'ien-*

*hou ti Chung-kuo cheng-chih* 辛亥革命前后的中國政治 (Chinese politics surrounding the Revolution of 1911). Peking, 1954. A rev. version of [164]. 2269/4342.111

[164] _____ . *Hsin-hai ko-ming yü Yüan Shih-k'ai* 辛亥革命與袁世凱(The Revolution of 1911 and Yüan Shih-k'ai). Hong Kong, 1948. 2269/4342.11        49, 122

[165] Li Tung-fang. *Hsi-shuo Ch'ing-ch'ao* 細說清朝(A detailed narration on the Ch'ing dynasty). 2 vols. Taipei, 1962.

[166] _____ . *Hsi-shuo Min-kuo* 細說民國 (A detailed narration on the Republic [of China]). 2 vols. have appeared. Taipei, 1966-. 2970/2350

[167] Liao Hsing-han. *Sun Wen ta-shih chi* 孫文大事記 (An outline of the life of Sun Yat-sen). 3rd ed. Shanghai, 1926. 4738.31/1964.784

[168] Lin Chih-tao, comp. *Ts'ai-fang hsin-hai Chiang-ning chu-fang hsün-nan hsing-shih piao* 採訪辛亥江寧駐防殉難行事表(A list of the [Ch'ing] officers of the Nanking troops martyred in 1911). Nanking, 1915. 2259.8/2304.1

[169] Lin Hsiung-hsiang, ed. *T'ai-wan sheng t'ung-chih kao* 台灣省通史稿 (A draft gazetteer of Taiwan province). 13 *chüan* have appeared. Taipei, 1951-. 3226/0.94     65, 102

[170] Lin Shu-ch'ing, *Chiang-tso yung-ping chi* 江左用兵記 (Military expedition to the north of the Yangtze). Chingkiang, 1928.

[171] Ling-nan Fen-weng, pseud., ed. *Hsin-hai Yüeh- luan hui-pien* 辛亥粵亂彙編 (A collection of materials on the Rebellion of 1911 in Kwangtung). Canton, 1911.             92

[172] Liu Hou-sheng. *Chang Ch'ien chuan-chi* 張謇傳記 (A biography of Chang Ch'ien). Shanghai, 1958; reprint, Hong Kong, 1965. 2269/1332.3

[173] Liu K'uei-i. *Huang Hsing chuan-chi* 黃興傳記 (A biography of Huang Hsing). Peking? 1929; reprint, Taipei, 1952. 4738.31/4878.1

[174] Liu Ta-wu, ed. *Ts'ai Sung-p'o hsien-sheng i-chi* 蔡松坡先生遺集(A posthumous compilation of

the writings of Ts'ai O). Chungking? 1943; reprint, Taipei, 1962. 2269/4982

[175] Liu Ya-sheng. *Chung-kuo min-tsu min-chu ko-ming yün-tung shih chiao-ch'eng* 中國民族民主革命運動史教程(A textbook history of the national and democratic revolutionary movement in China). Vol. 1, Yenan? 1941. 2744/7212                    100

[176] Lo Cheng-chün. *Hsin-hai hsün-chieh lu* 辛亥殉節錄 (The martyrdom of 1911). Hsiang-t'an, Hunan, 1920. 2259.8/6118

[177] Lo Chia-lun.*Ch'i-shih-nien lai Chung-kuo kuo-min-tang yü Chung-kuo*七十年來中國國民黨與中國 (China and the Chinese Nationalist Party of the past seventy years). Taipei, 1964.

[178] _____ . *Chung-shan hsien-sheng Lun-tun pei-nan shih-liao k'ao-ting* 中山先生倫敦被難史料考訂 (A critical study of the sources on the London kidnapping of Sun Yat-sen). Shanghai, 1930; Taipei reprint, 1971. 16, 27, 4738.31/1904.371                    127

[179] Lo Hsiang-lin. *Kuo-fu chia-shih yüan-liu k'ao*國父家世淵流考 (A study of the family origin of Sun Yat-sen). Chungking, 1942; reprint, Taipei, 1971. 4738.31/1904.26

[180] _____ . *Kuo-fu chih ta-hsüeh shih-tai* 國父之大學時代(The college life of Sun Yat-sen). Chungking, 1945; Taipei, 1971. 4738.31/1904.27                    38

[181] _____ . *Kuo-fu yü Ou Mei chih yu-hao* 國父與歐美之友好(Sun Yat-sen and his European and American friends). Taipei, 1951. 4738.31/1904.28

[182] Lo Kang. *Chung-hua min-kuo kuo-fu shih-lu ch'u-kao*中華民國國父實錄初稿(A draft version of the veritable records of the father of the Republic of China). Vol. 1, Taipei, 1965. 4738.31/1904.44                    71

[183] _____ . *Lo-pien Kuo-fu nien-p'u chiu-miu* 羅編國父年譜糾謬A critique of [74], *Kuo-fu nien-p'u ch'u-kao* [First draft of a *nien-p'u* of Sun Yat-sen] edited by Lo [Chia-lun]). Taipei, 1962. 4738.31/1904.73                    70

[184] Lu Chih-chih *et al.*, eds. *Ch'en Chiung-ming p'an-kuo shih* 陳炯明叛國史(The rebellion of Ch'en

Chiung-ming). Shanghai, 1922. Reprinted in [259], II-III.
2760/7996.2                                                     93

[185] Lu Man-yen, ed. *Chung-hua min-kuo k'ai-kuo ch'ien ko-ming wen-hsien* 中華民國開國前革命文獻 (Documents of the revolution preceding the founding of the Republic of China). 1944. 2960/7169         98

[186] Lu Pao-hsüan. *Man-ch'ing p'ai-shih* 滿清稗史 (A history of Manchu rule). 18 *ts'e*. Shanghai, 1914. 2746/7121         92

[187] Lu Tan-lin. *Ko-ming shih-hua* 革命史話 (Historical accounts of the Revolution). Shanghai, 1947. 2960/7174.1

[188] ———— . *Ko-ming shih-t'an* 革命史譚 (Historical accounts of the Revolution). Nanking, 1947. 2960/7174

[189] Lu Yu-pai, comp. *Sun Chung-shan hsien-sheng chuan-chi* 孫中山先生傳記 (Biographical writings on Sun Yat-sen). Shanghai, 1928? 4738.31/1904.14     95

[190] Mao Ssu-ch'eng, ed. *Min-kuo shih-wu-nien ch'ien chih Chiang Chieh-shih hsien-sheng* 民國十五年前之蔣介石先生 (The [early] career of Chiang Kai-shek, 1887-1926). 20 *ts'e*. N.p., 1937. 2269/4451.14     95

[191] Mao Tse-tung *et al. Sun Chung-shan: Chung-kuo jen-min wei-ta ti ko-ming ti erh-tzu* 孫中山：中國人民偉大的革命的兒子 (Sun Yat-sen: son of the great revolution of the Chinese people). Comp. by Tsou Sheng. Selection of articles overlapping contents of [192]. Hong Kong, 1957. 4738.31/1904.57     100

[192] ———— *et al. Wei-ta ti Sun Chung-shan* 偉大的孫中山 (Sun Yat-sen the Great). Hong Kong, 1957. 4738.31/1904.48     100

[193] Min Erh-ch'ang, comp. *Pei-chuan chi-pu* 碑傳集補 (A supplement to the collection of biographies). 24 *ts'e*. Peking, 1932. 2259.8/8524.2     94

[194] Miyazaki Torazo. *Ta ko-ming-chia Sun I-hsien* 大革命家孫逸仙 (Sun Yat-sen, the great revolutionary). Abridged trans. by Huang Chung-huang (Chang Shih-chao) from Miyazaki's *Sanjusannen no yume* 三十三年の夢 (The thirty-three years' dream).

Shanghai, 1903, 1906; reprint, Taipei, 1962. Published also as
Pai-lang t'ao-t'ien, pseud., *San-shih-san-nien lo-hua-meng*  15-16,
      (Thirty-three years' dream),   91
[Shanghai], 1925. 4738.31/1904.68

[195] Pai Chiao, pseud. *Yüan Shih-k'ai yü Chung-hua
min-kuo* 袁世凱與中華民國 (Yüan Shih-k'ai and
the Republic of China). Shanghai, 1936; reprint, Taipei,
1962. 2269/4342.1 & 2269/4342.1a

[196] P'an Kung-chan. *Ch'en Ch'i-mei* 陳其美
([The life of] Ch'en Ying-shih). Taipei, 1954. 4738.31/7948.2

[197] [Pao Kung-i] T'ien Hsiao-sheng, ed. *Chung-hua
min-kuo ta-shih chi* 中華民國大事記 (A chronicle
of the Republic of China). Shanghai, 1912.

[198] Pei Hua. *Chung-kuo ko-ming shih* 中國革
命史 (A history of Chinese revolution). Shanghai, 1928.
2960/6845

[199] P'eng Shu-chih. *Chung-kuo ko-ming ti ken-pen
wen-t'i* 中國革命的根本問題 (The basic issues
of the Chinese Revolution). N.p., 1928. 4292.1/4233   44

[200] Shang-hai-t'ung she, ed. *Shang-hai yen-chiu tzu-
liao hsü-chi* 上海研究資料續集 (A supplement
to the collection of sources for studies on Shanghai). Shanghai, 1936-39. 3069.23/2333

[201] Shang-hai tzu-yu-she, comp. *Chung-kuo ko-
ming-chi* 中國革命記 (Accounts of the Chinese
Revolution). 30 vols. Shanghai, 1911-12.   92

[202] Shang Ping-ho. *Hsin-jen ch'un-ch'iu* 辛壬春
秋 (Spring and autumn annals: 1911-12). 16 *ts'e*. N.p., 22, 67,
1924. Reprint, Taipei, 1962. 2960/9222   74, 94

[203] Shao Yüan-ch'ung. *Ch'en Ying-shih hsien-sheng
ko-ming hsiao-shih* 陳英士先生革命小史 (A bio-
graphical sketch of Ch'en Ch'i-mei). Shanghai, 1925? 4738.31/
7948.3

[204] Shen Yün-lung. *Chin-tai cheng-chih jen-wu lun-
ts'ung* 近代政治人物論叢 (Collected essays on
modern political figures). Taipei, 1965.   95, 96

[205] ———. *Hsien-tai cheng-chih jen-wu shu-p'ing*
現代政治人物述評 (Accounts and appraisals of

political figures in modern times). Hong Kong, 1959; rev. and enl. ed., Taipei, 1966. 2259.9/3110                                    75

[206] ――――― . *Li Yüan-hung p'ing-chuan* 黎元洪 評傳(A biography of Li Yüan-hung). Taipei, 1963. 2269/2313.21                                    75, 102

[207] Shih Chün. *Chung-kuo chin-tai shih-hsiang-shih ts'an-k'ao tzu-liao chien-pien* 中國近代思想史 參考資料簡編 (A selected collection of reference materials for the study of modern Chinese intellectual history). Peking, 1957. 4608/1624.1                                    100

[208] Shu Hsin-ch'eng. *Chin-tai Chung-kuo liu-hsüeh shih* 近代中國留學史 (A history of the Chinese who have studied abroad in modern times). Shanghai, 1927. 4911/8204.325

[209] Sun Wen. *Chung-kuo ko-ming shih* 中國 革命史 (A history of the Chinese Revolution). Canton, 1923. 2960/1904                                    18, 90

[210] ――――― . *Ko-ming yüan-ch'i* 革命緣起 (The origin of the Revolution). Originally written in 1918 as the concluding chapter of Sun's grand program for China's ideological revolution and reconstruction. While the program was simultaneously entitled ''Hsin-li chien-she'' 心理建設 (Ideological construction) and ''Sun Wen hsüeh-shuo'' 孫文學說 (The philosophy of Sun Yat-sen), the concluding chapter was originally entitled ''Yu-chih ching-ch'eng'' 有志竟成 (Where there is a will there is a way). This last chapter was published soon afterward in a single volume under the new title of *Ko-ming yüan-ch'i*. It was published still later in various editions under different titles, such as *Sun Chung-san hsien-sheng tzu-chuan* (Autobiography of Sun Yat-sen). For a good early edition of this work, see [215], I, *Autobiography:* 1-20. For an edition with detailed annotation, see [109]. 孫中山先生自傳                18-19, 38, 93, 116-17, 127

[211] ――――― . *Kuo-fu ch'üan-chi* 國父全集 (Collected works of Sun Yat-sen). Compiled by the Kuomintang Archive. Taipei, 1957; enl. ed., 3 vols, Taipei, 1965. 4738.10/1957                                    90, 127

[212] ――――― . *Kuo-fu ch'üan-shu* 國父全書 (Collected works of Sun Yat-sen). Ed. by Chang Ch'i-yün and others. Taipei, 1960. 4738.10/1960                                    90, 127

[213] _____ . *Sun I-hsien Lun-tun pei-nan chi* 孫逸仙倫敦被難記 (The London kidnapping of Sun Yat-sen). Shanghai, 1912; reprinted in Chia-i, Taiwan, 1945, and included in such collections as [211] and [215]. See [178] for a critical study of the work. 4738.31/1904.37    16

[214] _____ . *Sun Wen hsüeh-shuo* 孫文學說 (The philosophy of Sun Yat-sen). Shanghai, 1926. Several editions appeared. The item was reproduced also in collections such as [211] and [212]. Chapter VIII, an autobiography of Sun, has often been reproduced as a separate work (see additional bibliographic information under [210]). 4738.191/1927    126

[215] _____ . *Tsung-li ch'üan-chi* 總理全集 (Collected works of Sun Yat-sen). Comp. by Hu Han-min. 4 vols. Shanghai, 1930. Taipei reprint, 1965. 4738.10/1930a    90, 95, 126,27

[216] Sung Chiao-jen. *Ch'eng Chia-sheng ko-ming ta-shih lüeh* 程家檉革命大事畧 (A brief account of the revolutionary deeds of Ch'eng Chia-sheng) Mimeo. N.p., 1913.

[217] _____ . *Wo chih li-shih* 我之歷史 (An account of my life). T'ao-yüan, Hunan, 1920; reprint, Taipei, 1962. 2269/3942    21-22

[218] _____ , and Tai Chi-t'ao. *Sung Yü-fu Tai T'ien-ch'ou wen-chi ho-k'an* 宋漁父戴天仇文集合刊 (Works of Sung Chiao-jen and Tai Chi-t'ao). Shanghai, 1921. 2980/3942    127-28

[219] Sung-ch'ing-t'ang chu-jen, pseud., comp. *Hsin-hai Ssu-ch'uan lu-shih chi-lüeh* 辛亥四川路事紀略 (A brief account of the railway issue in Szechwan in 1911). Chengtu, Szechwan, 1915. 4500/0390

[220] Sung Yüeh-lun. *Tsung-li tsai Jih-pen chih ko-ming huo-tung* 總理在日本之革命活動 (The revolutionary activities of Sun Yat-sen in Japan). Taipei, 1953. 4738.31/1904.341

[221] Tai Chi-t'ao. *Tai T'ien-ch'ou wen-chi* 戴天仇文集 (Collected works of Tai Chi-t'ao). Taipei, 1962. A reproduction of [218]. In the preface of the Taipei reprint, the editor maintains that since all the writings in

this volume were the work of Tai, Sung Chiao-jen's name should therefore be omitted from the title. 2980/3942

[222] Tai Chih-li, comp. *Ssu-ch'uan pao-lu-yün-tung shih-liao* 四川保路運動史料 (Historical materials on the railway issue in Szechwan). Peking, 1959. 4500/4543                                                    51

[223] T'ao Ch'eng-chang. *Che-an chi-lüeh* 浙案紀略(A brief account of the [revolutionary] incidents in Chekiang). N.p., 1916. 2960/7250                                    21

[224] T'ao Chü-yin. *Liu chun-tzu chuan* 六君子傳 (The careers of six righteous men). Shanghai, 1946. 2259.9/7247                                                    128

[225] ————. *Pei-yang chün-fa t'ung-chih shih-ch'i shih-hua* 北洋軍閥統治時期史話 (The story of the rule of northern warlords). 6 volumes have appeared. Peking, 1957-. 2975/7247

[226] ————. *Yüan Shih-k'ai ch'ieh-kuo chi* 袁世凱竊國記 (Yüan Shih-k'ai betrayed his country). Taipei, 1954. A reproduction of [224]. 2259.9/7274a

[227] Teng Tse-ju. *Chung-kuo Kuo-min-tang erh-shih-nien shih chi* 中國國民黨二十年史蹟 (Historical materials on the Kuomintang). Shanghai, 1948.

[228] T'ien-ku, pseud. *Nan-pei ch'un-ch'iu* 南北春秋(Annals of the North and the South). Shanghai, 1912? 2960/1344                                                    92

[229] Ting Shih-yüan. *Mei-leng-chang-ching pi-chi* 梅楞章京筆記 (Notes of Ting Shih-yuan). Dairen, 1942.

[230] Ting Wen-chiang, ed. *Liang Jen-kung hsien-sheng nien-p'u ch'ang-pien ch'u-kao* 梁任公先生年譜長編初稿 (First draft of a detailed *nien-p'u* of Liang Ch'i-ch'ao). 3 vols. Taipei, 1958. Reprinted in the same title, bound with *K'ang Nan-hai p'i Liang Jen-kung shih-kao shou-chi* 康南海批梁任公詩稿手蹟 (Liang Ch'i-ch'ao's calligraphy of his own poems with Kang Yu-wei's annotative comments), ed. by Yang Chia-lo. 2 vols., Taipei, 1972. 2278/2934                                                    73

[231] Ts'ai Chi-ou, *O-chou hsüeh-shih* 鄂州血史 (A bloody nightmare of Hupeh province). Shanghai, 1958. 2960/4937

[232] Ts'ao Ya-po. *Wu-ch'ang ko-ming chen-shih* 武昌革命真史 (The true story of the Wuchang revolution). 3 vols. Shanghai, 1930. Partially reprinted in [2], 1:572-86 and 5:104-68. 2960/5612    31, 96

[233] Ts'en Ch'un-hsüan, *Lo-chai man-pi* 樂齋漫筆 (Recollections of Ts'en Ch'un-hsüan). Reprint, Taipei, 1962. 2269/2259

[234] Ts'en Hsüeh-lü, ed. *San-shui Liang Yen-sun hsien-sheng nien-p'u* 三水梁燕孫先生年譜 (A *nien-p'u* of Liang Shih-i). 2 vols. A reprint of [80], Taipei, 33, 114 1962. 2269/3940f

[235] Tso Shun-sheng. *Chung-kuo chin-tai-shih ssu-chiang* 中國近代史四講 (Four lectures on modern Chinese history). Hong Kong, 1962. 2744/4122

[236] _____ . *Hsin-hai ko-ming shih* 辛亥革命史 (A history of the Revolution of 1911). Shanghai, 1934.

[237] Tsou Lu. *Chung-kuo kuo-min-tang shih-kao* 中國國民黨史稿 (Draft history of the Chinese Nationalist Party). Shanghai, 1929. Rev. and enl. ed., 4 vols. 27, 37, Chungking, 1944, and Shanghai, 1949; reprint, Taipei, 1965. 45, 90, 4738.28/2226    98

[238] _____ . *Hui-ku-lu* 回顧錄 (Recollections. 2 vols. Nanking, 1947. Reprint, Taipei, 1970. 2269/2226.1    95

[239] _____ . *Hung-hua-kang ssu-lieh-shih chuan-chi* 紅花岡四烈士傳記 (The life of four martyrs at Red Flower Hill). Shanghai, 1927. 2961/2226

[240] _____ . *Kuang-chou san-yüeh erh-shih-chiu ko-ming shih* 廣州三月二十九革命史 (An account of the "March 29" Uprising in Canton). A slightly rev. ed. of [138], Changsha, 1939. 2961/2226.1    119

[241] Tsou Yai. *Tsou Yai liu-shih tzu-shu* 鄒崖六十自述 (Memoirs of Tsou Yai written at the age of sixty). N.p., n.d. 2269/2221

[242] Tu    Ch'eng-hsiang.   *Tsou   Jung*   鄒容 (Tsou   Jung).   Nanking,   1946.   Reproduced   in   [244]. 4738.31/2236

[243] ———— . *Tsou   Jung   chuan*   鄒容傳 (A   biography   of   Tsou   Jung).   Taipei,   1953.   For   additional   information   see   [243].   2259.9/4160

[244] Tu   Po-ping.   *Chung-kuo   tsui-chin   pa-shih-nien   lai   ti   ko-ming   yü   wai-chiao* 中國最近八十年來的革命與外交   (The   revolutionary   movement and   diplomacy   in   China   during   the   past   eighty   years). Shanghai,   1933.   2744/4133

[245] Tzu-hsü-tzu, pseud. *Hsiang-shih-chi* 湘事記(An account   of   events   in   Hunan).   2 vols. Peking,   1914.

[246] Wang   Kuang-ch'i,   comp.   and   tr.   *Hsin-hai   ko-ming   yü   lieh-ch'iang   t'ai-tu* 辛亥革命與列強態度 (The   Revolution   of   1911   and   the   responses   of   foreign powers).   Shanghai,   1929.   Reprint,   Taipei,   1972.   A compilation primarily   of   German   documents.

[247] Wang   Ts'an-chih.   *Ch'iu   Chin   ko-ming   chuan* 秋瑾革命傳(The   revolutionary   career   of   Ch'iu Chin).   Taipei,   1954.   4738.31/2811.3

[248] Wang   Ying-ch'i   *et al.*   *Kuan-yü   Sun   Chung-shan   ti   chuan-chi   ho   k'ao-cheng* 關於孫中山的傳記和考證(Biographies   of   and   studies   about   Sun   Yat-sen).   Taipei,   1965.   4738.31/1904.702

[249] Wang   Ying-ch'i.   *Sun   Chung-shan   chuan-chi* 孫中山傳記(A   biography   of   Sun   Yat-sen).   Shanghai, 1935. A Taipei reprint version is in [248],1-46.   4738.31/1904.53

[250] Wang   Yün-wu. *T'an wang-shih* 談往事 (Recollections).   Taipei,   1964.   2269/1111.1

[251] Wang   Yün-wu   *et al.*   *Wo   tsen-yang   jen-shih kuo-fu   Sun   hsien-sheng* 我怎樣認識國父孫先生 (How   I   made   the   acquaintance   of   Sun   [Yat-sen]).   Taipei,   1965.   4738.31/1904.75

[252] Wen   Kung-chih.   *Chung-hua   min-kuo   ko-ming ch'üan-shih* 中華民國革命全史   (A   comprehensive   history   of   the   revolution[-ary   movement]   for the   Republic   of   China).   Shanghai,   1929.

[253] ————          *Tsui-chin   san-shih-nien   Chung-kuo   chün-shih   shih* 最近三十年中國軍事史

(A military history of modern China: 1894-1927). 2 vols. Shanghai, 1929. Reprint, Taipei, 1962. 2970/0484    28

[254] Wu Chao-hsien. *Hsin-hai Chiu-chiang ch'i-i chi-shih* 辛亥九江起義紀實 (An account of the 1911 uprising in Kiukiang). Manuscript. 2960/2365    98

[255] Wu Ching-heng. *Kuo-fu nien-hsi yü hsing-i* 國父年系㫒行誼 (A chronicle and a sketch of the life of Sun Yat-sen). Taipei, 1952. 4738.31/1904.23

[256] ———— . *Kuo-fu Sun hsien-sheng nien-p'u* 國父孫先生年譜 (A *nien-p'u* of Sun Yat-sen). Chungking, 1940. 4738.31/1904.25

[257] ———— . *Tsung-li hsing-i* 總理行誼 (The life of Sun Yat-sen). Chungking, 1942, 1944. 4738.31/1904.23a

[258] ———— . *Wu Chih-hui ch'üan-chi* 吳稚暉全集 (Complete works of Wu Ching-heng). Shanghai, 1926. 5550/2349

[259] Wu Hsiang-hsiang, ed. *Chung-kuo hsien-tai-shih ts'ung-k'an* 中國現代史叢刊 (Collective writings on modern Chinese history). Taipei, 6 vols. have appeared since 1962. 2970/2343    72,74,76 102,124

[260] ———— . *Sun I-hsien hsien-sheng: Chung-hua min-kuo kuo-fu* 孫逸仙先生：中華民國國父 (Sun Yat-sen: The father of the Republic of China). Vol. 1, Taipei, 1965. Reprinted in 2 vols., Taipei, 1969. 4738.31/1904.33

[261] ———— . *Sung Chiao-jen: Chung-kuo min-chu hsien-cheng ti hsien-ch'ü* 宋教仁：中國民主憲政的先驅 (Sung Chiao-jen: The pioneer of the movement for China's democratic constitutional government). Taipei, 1965; reprint, 2 vols., Taipei, 1969. 2269/3942.1

[262] Wu I, ed. *Chung shan ko-ming shih* 中山革命史 (An account of the revolutionary activities of Sun Yat-sen). N.p., 1927. 4738.31/1904.34

[263] Wu T'ieh-ch'eng. *Wu T'ieh-ch'eng hui-i-lu* 吳鐵城回憶錄 (Memoirs of Wu T'ieh-ch'eng). Taipei, 1957; reprint, Taipei, 1966. 5236.9/1700

[264] [Wu T'ing-fang] Kuan-tu-lu, pseud. *Kung-ho kuan-chien lu* 共和關鍵錄 (The key documents to the founding of the Republic). Shanghai, 1912. 2960/4130    16, 96

[265] Wu T'ing-fang. *Wu Chih-yung hsien-sheng kung-tu* 伍秩庸先生公牘 (Papers of Wu T'ing-fang). 2 vols. Shanghai, 1913. 2269/2114.2

[266] Wu T'ing-hsieh. *Ho-fei chih-cheng nien-p'u* 合肥執政年譜 (A *nien-p'u* of Tuan Ch'i-jui). Tientsin? 1938; reprint, Taipei, 1962. 2279/7431

[267] Wu Tzu-hsiu. *Hsin-hai hsün-nan chi* 辛亥殉難記 (Martyrdom in 1911). Tientsin, 1916, 1921, 1923; enl. ed. comp. by Chin Liang, Tientsin? 1935. 2259.8/2304    23, 92

[268] Wu Yü-chang. *Hsin-hai ko-ming* 辛亥革命 (The Revolution of 1911). Peking, 1961. 2960/2310    52, 90, 100

[269] Yang-chou shih-fan hsüeh-yüan, Li shih hsi, ed. *Hsin-hai ko-ming Chiang-su ti-ch'ü shih-liao* 辛亥革命江蘇地區史料 (Historical materials on the 1911 Revolution in areas of Kiangsu). Nanking, 1961. 2960/4328    100

[270] *Yang Ch'ü-yün lüeh-shih* 楊衢雲略史 (Biographical sketch of Yang Ch'ü-yün). Hong Kong, 1927. 4738.31/4221

[271] Yang Shih-chi. *Hsin-hai ko-ming ch'ien-hou Hu-nan shih-shih* 辛亥革命前后湖南史事 (Historical events in Hunan surrounding the Revolution of 1911). Changsha, 1958. 2960/4247    100

[272] Yang Shih-ching. *Ch'ien Chiang-hsi kao-teng hsüeh-t'ang ko-ming yün-tung chih hui-i* 前江西高等學堂革命運動之回忆 (Reminiscent account of the revolutionary movement in the former Kiangsi Academy for Higher [Education]). Manuscript. 2960/4240    98

[273] ———. *Ch'ien Ching-shih ta-hsüeh-t'ang ko-ming yün-tung chih fu-liu chi ch'i shu-kuang* 前京師大學堂革命運動之伏流及其曙光 (Student unrest in the former Metropolitan Academy on the eve of the Revolution). Manuscript. 4180.1/4240

[274] Yang Sung and Teng Li-ch'ün, comps. *Chung-kuo chin-tai-shih chih-liao hsüan-chi* 中國近代史

資料逕輯(A selected collection of primary sources on modern Chinese history). Ed. by Jung Meng-yüan. Peking, 1954. 2748/4243.1                    100

[275] [Yang Tun-i] Su-min, pseud. *Man-i hua Hsia shih-mo chi* 滿夷滑夏始末記 (An account of the Manchu barbarian's rule of China). 11 vols. Shang-hai, 1912. Reprint, Taipei, 1969. 2960/1574                    17

[276] Yang Yü-ju. *Hsin-hai ko-ming hsien-chu-chi* 辛亥革命先著記(Recollections on the 1911 Revolution). Peking, 1958. 2960/4214

[277] Yao Yü-hsiang *et al*. *Yen-chiu Sun Chung-shan shih-liao* 研究孫中山史料 (Source materials on the career of Sun Yat-sen). Taipei, 1965. 4738.104/1335

[278] Yeh Ch'ang-chih. *Yüan-tu-lu jih-chi ch'ao* 緣督廬日記鈔 (Diaries of Yeh Ch'ang-chih). Comp. by Wang Chi-lieh. 16 *chüan*. Shanghai, 1933. 2268/4969

[279] Yeh Ch'u-ch'ang *et al*., eds. *Sung Yü-fu* 宋漁父 ([The life of] Sung Chiao-jen). 1962. Identical in content with [107], though on the cover of the Taipei reprint (1962) Yeh Ch'u-ch'ang is shown as chief editor.

[280] Yeh Hsia-sheng. *Kuo-fu Min-ch'u ko-ming chi-lüeh* 國父民初革命紀略(A brief account of the revolutionary activities of Sun Yat-sen in the early Republican period). Canton, 1948. 4738.31/1904.36                    93

[281] Yin Wei-lien. *Chung-kuo ko-ming shih* 中國革命史 (A history of the Chinese revolution). Shang-hai, 1929. 2744/7220

[282] Yü Han-ying, ed. *Chih-yüan chüeh-ssu-t'üan shih-mo chi* 志願決死團始末記(An account of the "Dare-to-Die" Volunteer Corps). Wuchang, 1913. 2960/8934                    92

[283] Yü Ping-chüan, ed. *Chung-kuo shih-hsüeh lun-wen yin-te* 中國史學論文引得(Index to historical articles in Chinese journals, 1902-62). Hong Kong, 1963. 9559/8924

[284] Yü Yu-jen *et al*. *Kuo-fu chiu-shih tan-ch'en chi-nien lun-wen chi* 國父九十誕辰紀念論文集

(Collected essays in commemoration of the ninetieth birthday of Sun Yat-sen). Vols. 1-2, Taipei, 1955; vol. 3, 1956. 4738.12/6844

[285] Yün Tai-ying. *Chung-kuo min-tsu ko-ming yün-tung shih* 中國民族革命運動史 (A history of the Chinese national revolutionary movement). N.p., 1926?

## JOURNALS

[286] *Chia-yin.* 甲寅, Tokyo, nos. 1-10 (May 1914-Oct. 1915). 9200/6300

[287] *Chiao-yü tsa-chih.* 教育雜誌' Shanghai, vol. 1, no. 1 - vol. 33, no. 12 (Jan. 1909-Dec. 1948). 4901/4000

[288] *Chien-kuo yüeh-k'an.* 建國月刊 Monthly. Shanghai, vol. 1, no. 1 - vol. 4, no. 4 (May 1927-Feb. 1931); and Nanking, vol. 4, no. 5 - vol. 17, no. 1 (March 1931 - July 1937). 9200/1672                 108

[289] *Chien-she.* 建設 Monthly. Shanghai, vol. 1, no. 1 - vol. 2, no. 6 (Aug. 1919-Aug. 1920). 4738.01/1404

[290] _____ . Weekly. Shanghai, nos. 1-9 (March-April 1926). 4738.01/1404.1

[291] *Chih-yen.* 制言 Semi-monthly. Soochow, nos. 1-47 (Sept. 1935-Aug.? 1937); then published as a monthly, Shanghai, nos. 48-62 (Jan. 1939-May? 1940). 9201/2206                 107

[292] *Chin-tai-shih tzu-liao* 近代史資料 Peking, no. 1 - (Aug. 1954-). 2748/3253                 51, 100

[293] *Ch'ing-hua chou-k'an* 清華週刊 Weekly. Peking, nos. 1-636 (March 1914-Jan. 1937). 4997.14/3245

[294] *Ch'ing-hua hsüeh-pao.* 清華學報 Quarterly. Peking, vol. 1, no. 1 - vol. 12, no. 3 (June 1924-July 1937). 9201/3474

[295] *Chuan-chi wen-hsüeh.* 傳記文學 Monthly. Taipei, Vol. 1, No. 1 - (June 1962- ). 2257.1/2007                 69, 72

[296] *Chung-hua yüeh-pao.* 中華月報 Monthly. Shanghai, vol. 1, no. 1 - vol. 4, no. 12 (March 1933-Dec. 1936). 9200/5474

[297] *Chung-kuo i-chou.* 中國一週 Weekly. Taipei, vol. 1, no. 1 - (May 1950- ). 9200/5617

[298] *Chung-yang jih-pao: Chung-yang fu-k'an.* 中央日報︰中央副刊 Daily. Taipei, 1 April 1949-. The Hoover East Asian Collection has a complete set of the newspaper without call number.

[299] *Fu-chien wen-hua.* 福建文化 Quarterly. Foochow, nos. 1-38 (Feb. 1931-March 1948). 9201/3102

[300] *Hsiang-tao chou-pao.* 响導週報 Weekly. Nos. 1-201 (Sept. 1922-July 1927). Tokyo reprint in 5 vols., 1963. For the various places of publication, see Tokyo reprint, vol. 5, Appendix pp. 10-14. 4292.01/2374                                          42, 99

[301] *Hsien-tai p'ing-lun.* 現代評論 Shanghai, nos. 1-209 (Dec. 1924-Dec. 1928). 9200-1200          91

[302] *Hsin Ch'ing-hai.* 新青海 Monthly. Nanking, vol. 1, no. 1 - vol. 5, no. 1 (Jan. 1933-Jan. 1937). 3079.6/0253

[303] *Hsin ch'ing-nien.* 新青年 Monthly. Shanghai, vol. 1, no. 1 - vol. 9, no. 6 (Sept. 1915-July 1922); quarterly, Canton, nos. 1-4 (June 1923-Dec. 1924), and nos. 1-4 (April 1925-May 1926). 9200/0258          99

[304] *Hsin Chung-hua.* 新中華 Semi-monthly. Shanghai, vol. 1, no. 1 - vol. 5, no. 15 (Jan. 1933-Aug. 1937); monthly, Chungking, new series, vol. 1-vol. 3, no. 12 (Jan. 1943-Dec. 1945); semi-monthly, Shanghai, vol. 4. no. 1-vol. 6, no. 24 (Jan. 1946-Dec. 1948). 9200/0254

[305] *Hsin Chung-kuo p'ing-lun yüeh-k'an.* 新中國評論月刊 Monthly. Taipei, vol. 1, no. 1 (Oct. 1950- ). 9200/0560          102

[306] *Hsin sheng-ming.* 新生命 Monthly. Shanghai, vol. 1, no. 1 - vol. 3, no. 12 (Jan. 1928-Dec. 1930). 9200/0228

[307] *Hsin shih-chi.* 新世紀 Weekly. Paris, nos. 1-52 (June 1907-May 1910). The title *Le Siècle Nouveau* was added to the cover from 23 Jan. 1909. Reprinted in 4 vols., Shanghai, 1947. 4296/0242 microfilm.          90

[308] *Hsüeh-shu chi-k'an.* 學術季刊　　　Taipei, vol. 1, no. 1 - vol. 6, no. 4 (Sept. 1952-June 1958). 9201/7222

[309] *I-ching.* 易經　　　Semi-monthly. Shanghai, nos. 1-36 (March 1936-Aug. 1937). 9200/3321　　　98

[310] *Jen-wen yüeh-k'an.* 人文月刊　　　Monthly. Shanghai, vol. 1, no. 1 - vol. 8, no. 10 (Feb. 1930-Dec. 1937); new series as a quarterly, Shanghai, vol. 1, nos. 1-4 (1947-48). 9200/8072

[311] *Ko-ming wen-hsien ts'ung-k'an.* 革命文獻叢刊　Nos. 5-7 (March-Sept. 1947). For nos. 1-4, see [334]. 4738.28/9559　　　99

[312] *Ku Chin.* 古今　　　Semi-monthly. Shanghai, nos. 1-57 (March 1942-Oct. 1944). 9200/4682　　　99

[313] *Ku-kung chou-k'an.* 故宮週刊　　Weekly. Peking, nos. 1-510 (Oct. 1929-April 1936). 6011/4332

[314] *Kuo-feng.* 國風　　　Semi-monthly Nanking, vol. 1, no. 1 - vol. 6, no. 12 (Sept. 1932-June 1935;) monthly, vol. 7, no. 1-vol. 8, no. 12 (July 1935-June 1937). 9201/6571

[315] *Kuo Shih Kuan kuan-k'an.* 國史館館刊 Quarterly. Nanking, vol. 1, no. 1-vol. 2, no. 1 (Dec. 1947- Jan. 1949). Reprinted in Hong Kong, 1967. 4738.31/6588　　2, 33-34, 97

[316] *Kuo-wen chou-pao.* 國聞週報　　Weekly. Tientsin, vol. 1, no. 1-vol. 14, no. 49 (July 1924-Dec. 1937). 9200/6734

[317] *Li-shih chiao-hsüeh.* 歷史教學 Monthly. Tientsin, no. 1 - (Jan. 1951- ). 2451/7547　　100

[318] *Li-shih yen-chiu.* 歷史研究　　Quarterly. 2, 54, 56, Peking, no. 1- (Feb. 1954- ). 2451/7513　　60, 63, 100-2

[319] *Lin-shih cheng-fu kung-pao* 臨時政府 公報 (Bulletin of the Provisional Government). Nanking, nos. 1-58. (29 Jan.-5 April 1912). Reprinted in Taipei, 1972. 4660.9/1084

[320] *Min-chu-ch'ao.* 民主潮　　　　Monthly. Taipei, vol. 1, no. 1 - (Oct. 1950- ). 4737.2/7403　　102

[321] *Min-li-pao.* 民立報　Daily. Shanghai, 11 Oct. 1910 - 4 Sept. 1913. (Complete set of original ed. in Hoover East Asian Collection.) Taipei reprint in 33 vols.　16, 91-92

[322] *Min Pao.* 民報　Tokyo, nos. 1-26 (Dec.

1905-Feb. 1910), and a supplement issue (May 1906).
Peking reprint bound in 8 vols., Taipei reprint in 4 vols. 44, 51,
4738.29/7444                                                                                    90, 99

[323] *Pao-hsüeh chi-k'an.* 報學季刊        Quarterly. Shanghai, vol. 1, nos. 1-4 (Oct. 1934-Aug. 1935).
9931/4721

[324] *Pu-erh-sai-wei-k'o.* 布爾塞維克
Shanghai, vol. 1, no. 1 - vol. 5, no. 1 (Oct. 1927-July
1932). 4292.01/4132

[325] *San-min-chu-i pan-yüeh-k'an.* 三民主義半
月刊        Semi-monthly. Chungking, vol. 1, no. 1 - vol.
11, no. 3 (July 1942-Oct. 1947). 4738.01/1708.3

[326] *San-min-chu-i yüeh-k'an.* 三民主義月刊
Monthly. Canton, vol. 1, no. 1 - vol. 7, no. 5 (Jan. 1933-
May 1936). 4738.01/1708.1

[327] *Shen-pao yüeh-k'an.* 申報月刊        Monthly.
Shanghai, vol. 1, no. 1-vol. 4, no. 12 (July 1933-Dec.
1935). 9200/5472

[328] *Shih-hsüeh chuan-k'an.* 史學專刊
Canton, vol. 1, no. 1 - vol. 2, no. 1 (Dec. 1935-Aug. 1937).

[329] *Ssu-ch'uan yüeh-pao.* 四川月報
Monthly. Chungking, vol. 1, no. 1 - vol. 11, no. 2 (July
1932-Aug. 1937). 4359.23/6274

[330] *Ssu-yü-yen.* 思與言        Taipei, vol. 1, no.
1—(May 1963-). 4001/6370

[331] *Ta-feng.*        大風        Hong Kong, nos. 1-59
(three issues a month), nos. 60-101 (two issues a month),
Mar. 1938-Nov. 1941. 9200/4371                                         98

[332] *Ta-lu tsa-chih.* 大陸雜誌        Semi-monthly. Taipei, vol. 1 - (July 15, 1950-). 9201/4700

[333] *Tang-i yen-chiu* 黨義研究        Semi-monthly. Kweilin, nos. 1-33 (Oct. 1941 - June? 1943), and vol.
4, no. 1 - ? (1943-?). 4738.01/9813

叢刊[334] *Tang-shih shih-liao ts'ung-k'an.* 黨史史料
叢刊 Irregular publication. Chungking, nos. 1-4
(1942?-1945). Published as [311] from no. 5 on.
4738.28/9559                                                                              99
[335] *Ti-hsüeh tsa-chih.* 地學雜誌        Monthly.

Peking, vol. 1, no. 1 - vol. 24, no. 1 (Jan. 1910-Jan. 1937). 3002/4700

[336] *Tung-fang tsa-chih.* 東方雜誌
Monthly. Shanghai, vol. 1, no. 1 - vol. 16, no. 12 (March 1904-Dec. 1919); semi-monthly, vol. 17, no. 1 - vol. 43, no. 24 (Jan. 1920-Dec. 1947); monthly, vol. 44, nos. 1-12 (Jan.-Dec. 1948). 9200/5000                                    91, 119

[337] *Wen-hsing.* 文星    Monthly. Taipei, nos. 1-98 (Nov. 1957-Dec. 1965). 9200/0461                              102

[338] *Yung-yen.* 庸言    Semi-monthly. Tientsin, vol. 1, nos. 1-24; monthly, vol.2, nos. 1-6 (Dec. 1912-June 1914). 9200/0206

[339] *Yüeh-feng.* 越風    Semi-monthly. Hang-chow, nos. 1-20 and vol. 2, nos. 1-4 (Oct. 1935?- 1937). 2451/4871

[340] *Yün-nan.* 雲南    Monthly.    Tokyo,    nos. 1-4 (Aug. 1906-Feb. 1907).    Nos. 1-3 reprinted in Taipei. Also reproduced in part as a single volume under the title *Yün-nan tsa-chih hsüan-chi*                (Selections from *Yün-nan*). Peking, 1958. 3075/1342

# Addenda

The year 1972 appears to be a good cutoff point for the biblio-graphic survey on the Revolution for two reasons. In the first place, there has been a complete blackout of publications on the subject from the Chinese Mainland since the Cultural Revolution. Secondly, the voluminous flow from Taiwan of reprints, compilations and monographic studies triggered by the government-sponsored cele-brations on the fiftieth anniversary of the Revolution and the centenary of Sun Yat-sen's birth subsided toward to the end of that year. The bibliography in this study, however, is based largely on research done in the sixties, with the round-the-world library searching done in 1966-67 and the manuscript brought to final form in 1969. In the process of updating the bibliography—both to absorb the better works from Taiwan and to include the recent acquisitions of the Hoover East Asian Collection of rare earlier editions—I have received generous and prompt assistance from scholars in Taiwan and at Hoover, in particular from Professor Li Yün-han. While it involved little alteration of the manuscript to incorporate the reprint data, new publications cannot be inserted in the Bibliography without affecting the entry-number series, which would in turn affect the entry-number citation in the text. In order to keep production cost at a minimum, the Addenda are provided herewith, following the same format as the Bibliography.

[341] Chang P'eng-yüan. *Li-hsien-p'ai yü hsin-hai ko-ming* 立憲派與辛亥革命 (The Constitutionalists and the Revolution of 1911). Taipei, 1969. 2920/1326    76

[342] Chang Wen-po. *Wu Chih-hui hsien-sheng chuan* 吳稚暉先生傳 (A biography of Wu Chih-hui). Enl. ed., 2 vols. Taipei, 1965; reprint, Taipei, 1969. 2944/0501

[343] Chang Yü-fa. *Ch'ing-chi ti li-hsien t'uan-t'i* 清季的立憲團體 (Constitutionalist organizations in the [late] Ch'ing period). Taipei, 1971. 4890.11/1313    76

[344] Ch'en T'ien-hsi. *Tai Chi-t'ao hsien-sheng pien-nien chuan-chi* 戴季陶先生編年傳記 (A biographical chronicle on Tai Chi-t'ao). Taipei, 1958. 2269/4527

[345] Ch'en Tsu-hua. *Yü Yu-jen hsien-sheng ch'uang-pan ko-ming-pao-k'an chih ching-kuo chi ch'i ying-hsiang* 于右任先生創辦革命報刊之經過及其影响 (Yü Yu-jen's efforts to establish revolutionary journals and their influences). Taipei, 1967. 9971/7934

[346] Cheng Lan-sun, *et al.*, eds. *Fu-chien hsin-hai kuang-fu shih* 福建辛亥光復史 (A history of the revolution in 1911 to restore the sovereignty of Fukien from the Manchu rule). Lien-ch'eng, Fukien, 1941. [A rare, war-time edition, with the publication data derived from its "Preface" and Chapter One.] 3072/7945    97

[347] Chou K'ai-ch'ing. *Min-kuo Ssu-ch'uan shih-shih* 民國四川史事 (Historical writings on Szechwan in the Republican period). Taipei, 1969.

[348] Chung-hua min-kuo hsin-hai Wu-ch'ang shou-i t'ung-chih hui, ed. *Wu-ch'ang ch'i-i* 武昌起義 (The Wuchang Uprising). 2 vols. Taipei, 1971. A revised and enlarged edition of Part II, vol. 1 of [57]. 2962/5476

[349] Chung-hua min-kuo shih-liao yen-chiu chung hsin, ed. *Chung-hua min-kuo shih-shih chi-yao (ch'u kao): Min-kuo yüan-nien i chih liu-yüeh* 中華民國史事紀要(初稿): 民國元年一至六月 (Historical chronicle of the Republic of China [preliminary version]: January-June, 1912). 2 vols. Taipei, 1971. 2970/5476.55

[350] Chung-kuo kuo-min-tang. Chung-yang tang-shih shih-liao pien-tsuan wei-yüan-hui, ed. *Huang K'o-ch'iang hsien-*

*sheng ch'üan-chi* (A complete collection of Huang Hsing). Taipei, 1968. 4378.31/4878.44

[351] _____ , ed. *Ko-ming jen-wu chih* 革命人物志 (Collective biographies of revolutionaries). 9 volumes have come out since 1969. Taipei. 2259.9/4882.03    66

[352] Chung-kuo lao-kung yün-tung shih pien-tsuan wei-yüan-hui, ed. *Chung-kuo lao-kung yün-tung shih* 中國勞工運動史 (A history of the Chinese labor movement). 5 vols. Taipei, 1959. 4460/5691

[353] Hsi Yün-chang. *Chung-hua min-kuo k'ai-kuo chi* 中華民國開國史(Founding of the Republic of China). Taipei, 1968.

[354] *Hu-pei wen hsien* she, ed. *Hsin-hai Wu-ch'ang shou-i shih-pien* 辛亥武昌首義試編(Compilation on the Wuchang Uprising of 1911). 2 vols. Taipei, 1971. 2960/2936

[355] Huang Kuang-hsüeh, ed. *Kuo-fu ko-ming i-shih* 國父革命逸史 (Anecdotes of Sun Yat-sen's revolutionary career). Taipei, 1965. 4738.31/1904.46

[356] _____ . *Kuo-fu Sun Chung-shan pen - chi* 國父孫中山本紀 (A biography of Sun Yat-sen). Taipei, 1951? [A rather rare earlier publication from Taiwan with date unascertainable from the Hoover copy.] 4738.31/1904.785

[357] Huang Shen I-yün. *I-yün hui-i* 亦雲回憶 (Memoirs of [Huang Shen] I-yün). 2 vols. Taipei, 1968. 2209/4822.01    103

[358] Kuo T'ing-i, ed. *Chin-tai Chung-kuo shih-shih jih-chih* (A day-to-day chronicle on modern China). 2 vols. Taipei, n.d.

[359] Li Tsung-huang. *Li Tsung-huang hui-i-lu: Pa-shih-san-nien feng-tou shih* 李宗黃回憶錄:八十三年奮鬥史 (Memoirs of Li Tsung-huang: A career of eighty years of struggle). 2 vols. Taipei, 1972. 2269/4434.43

[360] Liu Feng-han. *Yü Yu-jen nien-p'u* 于右任年譜 (A *nien-p'u* of Yü Yu-jen). Taipei, 1967. 2279/7474

[361] Liu Yüeh-sheng, ed. *Hsiang-kang Chi-tu chiao-hui shih* 香港基督教會史(A history of Christian

missions in Hong Kong). Hong Kong, 1941. 1982.5/7224

[362] Ting-wei Huang-kang shou-i liu-shih chou-nien chi-nien hui, ed. *Ting-wei Huang-kang shou-i liu-shih chou-nien chi-nien chuan-chi* 丁未黃岡首義六十周年紀念專集 (A special collection in commemoration of the sixtieth anniversary of the Huang-kang Uprising of 1907). Taipei, 1967. 2960/1547

[363] Tso Shun-sheng. *Huang Hsing p'ing-chuan* 黃興 評傳 (A biography of Huang Hsing). Taipei, 1968. 2269/ 4878.47

[364] Wu Hsiang-hsiang. *Min-kuo pai-jen-chuan* 民國 百人傳 (Collective biographies of one hundred Republican figures). 4 vols. Taipei, 1971. 2259.9/2343.76

[365] Yen Hsi-shan. *Yen Hsi-shan chao-nien hui-i-lu* 閻錫山早年回憶錄 (Yen Hsi-shan's reminiscent accounts of his early career). Taipei, 1968. 2269/7282.78          72

## JOURNALS

[366] *Chiang-su wen-hsien.* 江蘇文獻 Monthly. New series: no. 1— (July 1967— ). 3095/3102          70

[367] *Hu-pei wen-hsien* 湖北文獻 Monthly. Taipei, no. 1 - (Oct. 1966- ). 3069/3402          70

[368] *Ssu-ch'uan wen-hsien.* 四川文獻 Monthly. Taipei, no. 1— (Sept. 1962— ). 3064/6202          70

# Subject Index

This comprehensive subject index is designed to maximize access to the data contained in this volume, and hence to enhance the value of the book as a research guide to sources on the 1911 Revolution. The subject entries in this Index cover all major subjects not listed in the Table of Contents, and include Chinese calligraphy for the most significant Chinese and Japanese author names contained in text, Notes, and Bibliography, as well as titles of some significance that appear in the text or Notes but not in the Bibliography. For each entry, when applicable, references are made first to the text (by page numbers), then to the Notes section (by page numbers *and note numbers* ), and finally to the Bibliography (by entry numbers, in brackets). Major entries with numerous references are broken down into analytical subcategories.

The listing also provides numerous cross-references to guide the reader to related subjects and to clarify possible confusion caused by personal, institutional, and geographical name variations. Thus, if the reader seeks references to the revolutionary movement in Kiangsu province, for example, he need only look under the subject heading "provinces, revolutionary movement in," to find not only seven general references — one in the text (p.22), one in the Notes (pp. 99-92n.15), and five in the Bibliography ([2], [57], [145], [202], [253]) — but also the subcategory "Kiangsu," which directs him to seven specifically relevant subjects: "Chang Ch'ien," "Ch'en Ch'i-mei," "Chiang-su" (a geographical name variation), "Huang Fu," "Huang Shen I-yün," "Shanghai," and "Su Pao case," A check under all of these subject headings will in turn lead to a total of thirty-three different references in this volume, including ten in the text, eight in the Notes, and fifteen in the Bibliography.

Academia Sinica. *See* Chung-yang yen-chiu-yüan

Ah Ying 阿英   (pseud.). *See* Ch'ien Hsing-ts'un

Ai-hsin-chüeh-lo P'u-i 爱新覺羅溥儀   (Henry Pu-Yi, Hsüan-t'ung Emperor), 52, [1], [45]

Army for National Independence. *See* Tzu-li chün

*Asahi shimbun* 朝日新聞   (*Asahi Daily*, Tokyo), [130]


Beasley, W.G., 89n.1

Bergère, Marie-Claire, 8, 90n.7

   quoted, 8

Bolshevik Revolution, 6, 11, 43

bourgeoisie and capitalism, 8, 10, 11, 12, 42, 43, 47, 56-57, 60-61, 83, 99n.73

Boxers, 60, 61, 83


Canton Uprising (1911). *See* "March 29" Uprising

Ch'ai Te-keng 柴德賡 , 51, [2]

Chang Chi 張繼 , 72, [3]

Chang Ch'i-yün 張其昀 , [4], [5]

Chang Chiang-ts'ai 張江裁 , [7], [6]

Chang Ch'ien 張謇 , 26, 33, 57, 96n.48, [11], [12], [172]

Chang Ching-lu 張靜廬 , 53, [8], [9], [10]

Chang Fu-jui 張馥蕊 , 76

Chang Hsiao-jo 張孝若 , [11], [12]

Chang Hsing-yen 章行嚴 , 90n.10, [13]

Chang Huang-ch'i 張篁溪 , 26, 95n. 34

Chang K'ai-mei 張開枚 , [14]

Chang K'ai-yüan 章開沅 , 56-57

Chang Kuo-kan 張國淦 , [15]

Chang Nan 張枬 , [16]

Chang Nan-hsien 張難先 , 35-36, 37, 98n.67, [17]

# Other Hoover Books on China

## A Chinese-English Dictionary of Communist Chinese Terminology

*Dennis J. Doolin and Charles P. Ridley.* 1973. This 17,000-entry dictionary translates terms created or adapted by the Chinese Communist Party, with emphasis on recent years. Political terminology is stressed, but the dictionary also includes translations of a wide variety of proper names.

P124. 569 p. Hard, $27.50

## The Making of a Model Citizen in Communist China

*Charles P. Ridley, Paul H. B. Godwin, and Dennis J. Doolin.* 1971. The product of a research project for the United States Department of Health, Education, and Welfare, this book shows how the Chinese Communists use their educational system to mould what they consider model citizens.

P103. 401 p. Hard. $9.95

## China's Nation-Building Effort, 1927-1937

The Financial and Economic Record

*Arthur N. Young.* 1971. Written by the former Financial Adviser to China, this is a study of the economic and financial steps taken by the National Government of China during the critical decade 1927-37 to build China into a modern, viable nation.

P104. 553 p. Hard, $19.50

## The Petroleum Industry of the People's Republic of China

*H. C. Ling.* Forthcoming. Evaluates key factors of demand, including national defense, and supply, including transportation, technology, resources, and the institutional framework. Concludes that demand will not outstrip supply in the foreseeable future.

P142. 250 p. Price not set.